DO JUST ONE THING

DO JUST ONE THING

365 Ideas for a Better You, Life, and Planet

DANNY SEO

FOREWORD BY HARRY CONNICK JR.

Countryman Press

An Imprint of W. W. Norton & Company
Independent Publishers Since 1923

CONTENTS

FOREWORD

WHEN DANNY REACHED OUT and asked me to write the foreword to his book, I was honored. After seeing how talented he was on television; with his magazine, *Naturally, Danny Seo*; and on his social media accounts, it came as no surprise that he would author a book—and what a fantastic book it is!

If you're like me, you'll have two copies of *Do Just One Thing*, one for your home and an online version to refer to whenever you have a question about something. And, yes, if you "do just one thing," read this book. You and our planet will be better for it!

A little backstory...

The first time Danny stopped by as a guest on my daytime show, *Harry*, he taught me how to make cauliflower ice cream. I'm all about clean eating, but I'm also from New Orleans where cauliflower and ice cream aren't usually mentioned in the same sentence. However, because Danny was so charming, so engaging, and so qualified to speak about all things life-bettering, I watched and listened. I remember joking around a lot with Danny, teasing him. He laughed and smiled that infectious smile and never once was thrown off his game. He just continued making that cauliflower ice cream. I thought, *This guy is amazing. The audience loves him, I love him . . . I'm gonna like this ice cream whether I want to or not!* What's really crazy? I actually loved it, and it was a simple tip I could use to make plant-based, dairy-free ice cream. Better for me, and the planet!

We all looked forward to Danny's appearances on the show. Everyone got so excited for his giveaway shows—Holiday Giveaway, Earth Day Giveaway, Valentine's Day Giveaway—it was a highlight for all of us. I was impressed with both his expertise and his ability; he always taught us something useful.

I've stayed in contact with Danny over the years. I follow him on social media and keep up with his career, picking up life tips along the way. I'm always happy to see him on television and so proud of his ever-growing list of accomplishments. It couldn't happen to a nicer guy.

I am obsessed with this book and all the simple, ingenious tips Danny offers! Seriously—wait till you read it!

—Harry Connick Jr.

INTRODUCTION

WHERE DO I START? Figuring out the answer to that question is undoubtedly the biggest hurdle people face when they want to be a little greener, act a little kinder to the planet, and live a little more altruistically.

For more than 30 years, I've been dedicated to helping people learn all about eco-friendly living through my books, TV shows, and magazine. In my experience, getting over that hurdle is really about overcoming a sense of being overwhelmed. I think a lot of us live in an "all or nothing" mentality—but that attitude isn't a healthy one when it comes to striving to leave a lighter footprint in life. Making drastic lifestyle transformations overnight rarely leads to sustainable change. So, as people continued to ask me that question—Where do I start?—the phrase "Do Just One Thing" came to mind. I would share quirky but real tips with them, and they loved them. It all snowballed from there.

In 2009, I began penning a daily column called "Do Just One Thing" for Universal Syndicate to share my green-minded, money-saving, and waste-free ideas. A big takeaway over the years is that, yes, going green is the right thing to do to save the planet, but there are benefits to the doer as well. Saving energy means saving money; eating with less waste often means healthier food and a better sense of wellness. Even being mindful of what you buy resets the mind to think about how things don't really spark joy (wink, wink, Marie Kondo), and happiness can come from experiential activities like a good meal, a visit to a museum, or a hike through the woods.

Nearly 15 years later, I've written thousands of tips. When I started out, the goal was never to suggest buying more stuff. These tips don't require more things. Sure, investing in a new electric car is far better than driving a gas-guzzling SUV, but that suggestion is incredibly out of touch and—let's face it—we all know that. Nobody needs a syndicated column to state the obvious. Instead, my "Do Just One Thing" ideas were designed to make the reader think: *Who knew?* I actually channel the 1980s TV spy MacGyver when writing them, so that a sense of resourcefulness resonates.

Some ideas have gone viral. For example, I suggested a DIY idea where you store natural wine corks in a jar and fill it with rubbing alcohol. The next time you need a firestarter for the grill or fireplace, just grab one and light it. The alcohol-soaked cork creates a slow, even burn and is far better than using a chemical firestarter. This idea was shared by millions of people online (and this was before the age of TikTok and Instagram!). I even heard the tip shared on radio and TV shows. The reason I think it went viral is this: it's an interesting idea that anyone can do.

And that's the big idea behind this book: *anyone* can do *any one* of these tips. There are 365 ideas here to live greener, cut waste, help animals and wildlife, and do meaningful things for your community. Consider these my evergreen, all-star "Do Just One Thing" tips that I consider my go-to life hacks and habits. You can treat it like a calendar and try something each day or just dog-ear the ones you love. There's something for everyone here, and, yes, I would love for you to share your favorites with others. Who knows? You might see a nice bump of savings in your wallet, feel a little healthier, and just gain a sense of optimism overall about the whole world around you.

Just by reading this book, you've made the first step on a new journey. Now keep reading, and let's take small steps together to make a huge difference.

CHAPTER 1

A HEALTHY, HAPPY HOME

Now more than ever, we're spending a lot of time at home. And it doesn't really matter where you live or how large your home is, I think we can agree that we all want a place that is healthy to be in and as energy-efficient as possible. Taking smarter steps to improve your home health isn't just better for the planet and ourselves, it can also reap significant savings on your utility bills and can even help you avoid costly repairs down the road.

These are a mix of helpful hacks, truly easy DIY ideas, and a bunch of "who knew" tips to help you transform your abode into a lean, green, healthy, happy home.

1. PAINT PERFECT

If you only need a little bit of leftover house paint to save for touch-up down the road, try this upcycling idea: use old plastic water bottles. Start with a clean and dry water bottle and place a funnel on the top. Pour leftover paint into the bottle until it's about 95 percent full; remove the funnel, and toss in about 6 glass marbles. Tightly put the cap back on and secure it with a few strips of painter's tape. When it's time to use the paint, shake it; the marbles will blend the paint and you'll be good to go to paint in the future.

2. BOX IT UP

According to the US Department of Energy, about 14 percent of total air filtration in a home enters through a fireplace chimney. Cold drafts can enter a chimney even if the flue is pulled shut, which can make your home less energy-efficient in the winter months. There are products in the marketplace called chimney balloons that are nearly indestructible balloons you place inside the chimney to act as draft dodgers. They work to stop the cold drafts but can be expensive. One DIY solution? Rip open a cardboard box and tape it inside the chimney as a draft stopper. It will do the trick and help you save up to 30 percent on your heating bill. Just remember this: if you want to use the fireplace, be sure to remove the box first.

3. THE DISH

Here's a simple way to save water: Stop prerinsing all your dishes and cups before you put them in the dishwasher. Modern dishwashers today are designed to be as energy-and water-efficient as possible, so they are a much greener option than washing by hand. But the dishwashing tablets we use today are also far more effective than detergents from the past. The tablets use formulations that activate when they interact with grease, grime, and food debris on your dishes. If your dishes are too clean, the excess detergent will actually attack the top rack glassware, leaving scratches and marks on them. Technically, this tip will keep your dishes in tip-top shape for longer, and it will save you water!

4. PAINT CHIPS

If you live in an older home that was painted with lead-based paints, don't reach for the vacuum when paint begins to chip and peel off. While it may seem like a logical idea to use a vacuum if you're not touching the lead-based paint chips, contamination can occur when you open the vacuum to empty out the canister. Powerful vacuums can turn lead chips into dust, and when the canister is open, dust microparticles can contaminate the air in your home. Instead, clean up the lead-based chips using a manual dustpan and broom and throw them away in the trash.

5. SPICE IT UP

Parents who set up a little sandbox in their backyard as a place for their kids to play may also unknowingly be setting up the perfect environment for insects to nest and build colonies, too. Instead of reaching for chemical pesticides to keep your sandbox insect-free, head to your pantry instead. Generously sprinkle cinnamon all over the sandbox and rake it through the sand. The reason? Cinnamon is a natural insect deterrent, it's safe, and it smells nice, too! If you need a lot of cinnamon for an extra large sand-box, look for generic brands or inexpensive bulk containers at your local warehouse club store. Sprinkle away!

6. AIR IT OUT

When installing new carpet in a home, that new "smell" that comes from carpet is actually something called a volatile organic compound, or a VOC. The VOCs come from the glues and dyes used to make the carpet and can lead to poor indoor air quality when you install new carpet in your home. One way to help lessen your exposure to VOCs is to ask the carpet installer to unroll and air out the carpet for 48 hours at their warehouse before bringing it to your home. This pre-off-gassing will help significantly reduce the number of VOCs released in your house. Better yet: look for natural fiber carpets like sisal and wool, which have few to no VOCs.

7. SPIT IT OUT

Do you use mouthwash on a regular basis and just spit it down the bathroom sink? Take advantage of the disinfecting properties of mouthwash and do this instead: spit it out into the toilet. Let it sit in the water for about 30 minutes and then flush. The mouthwash will neutralize germs and actually leave a fresh, minty smell, too. If you want full maximum cleaning power, pour ¼ cup of mouthwash into the toilet and swish it around with a brush. However you use it, using mouthwash is a great way to get double disinfecting duty in the morning.

8. CLEAN IT UP

Ever get a greasy stain on clothes and worry that simply washing it in the washing machine won't do the job? Or worse, you just toss it into the trash to send it to the landfill? One might think to grab laundry detergent and try to spot clean the stain, but don't: most detergents are super-concentrated and are designed to work with water. They have very strong stain-fighting enzymes that, when applied directly to clothes, can create more damage and noticeable wear. Instead, reach for the best grease-cutting soap there is: dish soap. It's gentle, works to break up stains, and won't harm fabrics or clothes. Just spot treat, let it soak, and wash normally in the washing machine.

9. TRY THIS DRY

We separate our whites from colored clothing when we wash them, but when it comes to drying clothes, separate them according to weight. By drying heavy clothes (like jeans, sweaters, and thick flannel shirts) separately from light fabrics (T-shirts, undergarments), you can efficiently dry clothes using the least amount of energy. Start by drying a load of light fabrics first; they will dry quickly and warm up the inside of the dryer. Then add the heavier items for a second load; the residual heat from the first load will help speed up that drying process.

10. SO SHADY

Here's a one-time green thumb fix that will have a long-term effect on your air conditioning bills and carbon footprint: plant some ivy at the base of your house. Allowing ivy vines to crawl up the walls of your house provides a natural buffer between your home and the hot sun in the same way a shaded tree keeps your home cool. The ivy plant absorbs heat and thrives from the sun's rays and reduces reflection on your home to keep it cooler. Ivy is also an easy-to-grow plant that thrives almost with no upkeep after you plant it.

11. SLEEP TIGHT

Switching your cotton bedding over to organic cotton linens is not only more attainable today than it was several years ago, but it can have other benefits, too. Buying organic cotton bedding helps support farmers who grow organic cotton, and it also helps eliminate unnecessary chemicals from your lifestyle. Conventional cotton bedding is often bleached and then dyed using heavy metal dyes that can have formaldehyde resins. And if you choose sheets that are labeled "wrinkle-free," keep in mind that they are also treated with a chemical substance that has been linked as a suspected carcinogen. If you can't find organic cotton sheets, look for light-colored bedding that is not wrinkle-free for the next best (healthiest) thing.

12. PERFECT PAINT

Thinking about giving the outside of your house a fresh paint job? The color of the paint you choose can have a big impact on how energy-efficient your home can be. Homes in a warmer climate that choose a lighter color can increase their light reflective value (LRV). For example, a pure black color measures 0 percent LRV and a pure white has a 100 percent LRV. By choosing a lighter tint, you reflect light away and your home uses less energy to stay cool. For homes in more predominantly colder climates, a darker color can help absorb heat and reduce heating costs.

13. ROCK SOLID IDEA

If investing in a pricey dehumidifier to help remedy a damp room isn't in the budget, try this simple idea to draw moisture out of a room: use rock salt. The same deicing salt used on driveways in the wintertime can help pull moisture out of the air. All you have to do is drill some holes in the bottom of a small bucket and fill it up with rock salt. Place it inside a larger bucket and put it in the damp room. Over time, water will collect in the small bucket and drip into the larger one. Empty when it's full of water.

14. GET STONED

For many people, when doing a kitchen renovation, the dream is to have marble or granite countertops in the kitchen. But many exotic stones come from faraway places like Italy and South America, where these very heavy slabs have to be trucked, shipped, and retrucked. All this transportation burns up a tremendous amount of fossil fuel (not to mention the environmental devastation of the areas the solid surfaces are mined from). But if you must have stone countertops, think local. Look for locally quarried stone that came from your state; not only is it more carbon-neutral because it doesn't have to travel far distances, it's usually cheaper, too.

15. WATER WORKS

When washing your hands with soap and water, do your hands feel "slimy" after you've washed them? Or when it comes to cleaning clothes, do you have to use more laundry detergent than you've normally done in the past? This might be a sign your tap water is too "hard." When you have hard tap water, it means there's a buildup of minerals like calcium and magnesium. And while hard water is not necessarily bad for you, it could be an indication there are things like aluminum, manganese, and lead in your water, which means you should have your water tested for safety.

16. KEEP IT DRY

Ever find those little silica gel packets when you buy something new, like a new computer, a wicker basket, or even a bottle of vitamins? They are designed to absorb moisture and protect items from rust, but they are also nearly impossible to recycle. The good thing is that they have a million uses around the house. Leave them in a box of old photos, baseball cards, or any paper matter to prevent humidity from attacking printed items. Leave some inside toolboxes and camera bags to prevent rust on expensive equipment. If you save seeds to plant in spring, drop a few packets in with the seeds to protect them from mold during the fall and winter months.

17. TEST YOUR TAP

It can be nearly impossible to tell from just taste and smell if the water coming out of your tap is safe to drink. But confirming your tap water is safe can save you a lot of money from purchasing unnecessary water filters. The good news is, if your home uses public or municipal water lines, your water provider can give test results for the water for free. Just look up your water bill and call the supplier. The public water must be tested on a regular basis, and they must offer customers something called a Consumer Confidence Report, which details the results of the testing. The Environmental Working Group also maintains the EWG Tap Water Database. Just type in your zip code and you'll see a complete list of contaminants found in your city's water supply. Learn more at ewg.org/tapwater.

18. PERFECT PLACEMENT

Many of us know not to place a refrigerator next to heat sources like an oven, but did you know you should also avoid a sunny spot in your kitchen, too? Because radiant heat that comes from the sun through your windows is warm, when that sun's rays hit your refrigerator, it warms up, too. If your refrigerator/freezer warms up, it needs to work extra hard (using extra energy) to keep things cool and frozen inside. By avoiding sun spots or drawing the blinds down to block sun from hitting your fridge, you can save energy with this one easy step.

19. BREEZE THROUGH SUMMER

To keep your home cool during summer without turning on the AC, open the right windows in your home. According to the Natural Resources Defense Council, open low windows just a little bit on the windy side of the house and open the windows wide on the opposite side. This will draw cool air through the home with a tunnel effect, creating a cooling breeze.

20. SHOWER POWER

What's one way to save over 100 bucks and 4,600 gallons of water a year? Just shut off the shower when you are shampooing and conditioning your hair. A typical shower uses around 17 percent of the average household use of water (second biggest water hog in the home), so just turning off the shower valve when shampooing for just one minute can cut down on both energy (hot water) and water usage.

21. DIRTY DISHES

To hand wash or use the dishwasher? That is the question. According to the Environmental Protection Agency, using an Energy Star–qualified dishwashing machine is the eco winner. By going automated, you can save money on your utility bill, 230 hours of time normally spent hand-washing pots and pans, and up to 5,000 gallons of water a year. It all adds up to a huge reduction in greenhouse gases and conserves water.

22. SURGE PURGE

One of the biggest energy hogs in the home isn't glaringly obvious: the cable box/internet modem/wifi router. Designed to provide television, phone, and internet, the box is a major energy drain in itself. One way to help curb the cost of electricity is to plug the cable box into a surge protector that has an electrical kill switch. If you switch off the electricity right before you go to sleep and turn it back on in the morning, you'll reduce your household's overall energy usage by as much as 10 percent. Manufacturers like Belkin even make surge protectors with a remote control, so that one click can turn off the power to the cable box and other electronics plugged into the power strip.

23. PLANT STRATEGICALLY

Planting trees in the yard is one of the simplest ways to add value to your home and create future energy savings, too. Given that trees provide shade and shaded air is cooler, strategically plant trees so they provide shade wherever your air conditioning unit is. The reason is simple: the cooler air the unit draws in means it uses less energy to circulate air conditioning around the house. On the south side of your home, avoid putting in plants that can grow too tall. These tall plants can block sunlight in the winter months, which means your home can't take advantage of the ambient light and heat. And all around the house, plant dense evergreen shrubs. They look good all year-round and also naturally insulate to protect your home from the cold air outdoors.

24. SELF-CLEANING

The next time you make a roast or bake up a batch of cookies in your oven, don't let the hot air inside go to waste. After you've removed whatever you're cooking, give the inside of the oven a liberal spray of a water-and-white-vinegar solution. Do this quickly and shut the door. And let it sit for 30 minutes. As the vinegary solution evaporates, the inside will steam and help loosen up stubborn stains and marks. After 30 minutes (or when it's cool enough inside), just use a sponge or microfiber towel to wipe up the greasy mess.

25. LIGHT THE WAY

Some of us might try to avoid light emitting diode (LED) bulbs when lighting our homes because we're afraid that the light emitted will feel cold and clinical. But LED bulbs are highly energy-efficient, and finding the right bulbs can make all the difference in keeping your home warm and inviting. When shopping for LED bulbs, key words to search for are "warm white" or "soft white" on the packaging. But more importantly, look for kelvin ratings—a metric to measure color temperature—on the packaging. LED bulbs that are 3,000 kelvins or less cast a yellow light; any higher, and it'll likely be that cooler, bright white light.

26. CLEAR THE AIR

Air filters are needed components for almost all heating and cooling systems to capture dirt, dust, bacteria, and other debris and to keep the indoor air quality of your home healthy. But traditional disposable filters (which are made from a polyester fiber) are not recyclable and need to be replaced often. If throwing out filters concerns you, consider investing in reusable filters. While the reusable ones cost 10 times more, they can last several years, which will help you recoup the investment. The reusable ones are washable and just need to be thoroughly dried before you put them back into your heating/cooling system.

27. WARM UP TO THIS

Those little disposable hand warmers may not be recyclable or rechargeable, but there is a way to reuse them after they've kept your hands toasty. The hand warmers are made with nontoxic ingredients, and one of them is activated carbon, which is a natural deodorizer. Given that the mesh pouches let air through (they activate when exposed to cold air), they'll also absorb other things like odors! So toss some used hand warmers into smelly shoes to give them a freshening up.

28. PURIFYING FLORA

Houseplants offer another easy and effective way to detoxify and purify the air in your home. In fact, you can even use them to customize air purification for different rooms. For the bedroom, try a low maintenance Christmas cactus; it looks pretty, removes CO_2 at night, and releases oxygen during the day, so it purifies as you sleep. For the living or family room, go with palm trees; not only do decorators like their look, but they are also purifying workhorses that remove ammonia from cleaning products and help add moisture to dry air. And for your home office, go with the pothos plant; it can thrive despite neglect after long weeks, and its favorite thing to absorb? Formaldehyde. This one turns your work desk into a healthy haven.

29. SAFELY SPRINKLE

You need only raid your kitchen pantry to create an easy all-natural insect repellant to keep your potted plants and freshly planted seedlings in the garden from being attacked by pests. Grab cayenne pepper and garlic powder and sprinkle them around the plant and on top of the soil. This makes a perfectly harmless all-natural additive that won't hurt plants but insects hate. You can also boil water with garlic to make a garlic spray; when cool, pour the mixture into a bottle to spray leaves, stems, and anywhere you think insects may be attacking your plants.

30. COOL BULBS

Here's one more reason to consider investing in energy-efficient LED light bulbs for your home: they won't mess with your thermostat. Incandescent, halogen, and even CFL bulbs emit heat when they are turned on. If you have a lamp with one of these bulbs near your thermostat, it will sense the heat and assume that's the temperature of the room. In winter, it will keep the house too cold, and in summer, it will overwork to keep the house cool. With LED bulbs, you get the benefits of clean, bright light but with zero heat because LED bulbs do not produce heat and stay cool to the touch.

31. PATCH-UP POOL TOYS

Almost all inflatable toys for the pool or beach—balls, rafters, and floaties—have one thing in common: they are made from hard-to-recycle polyvinyl chloride or PVC plastic. But if your old pool toys are punctured and won't inflate, that doesn't mean you have to toss them in the trash. Look for PVC repair adhesive at your sporting goods store to fill small punctures and holes in minutes. It's also useful on camping equipment like tents, which can seal up a tear or hole to make your tent water-resistant for unexpected rain showers.

32. PLANT POWER

Many of us know not to flush old prescription pills and medications down the toilet, given that pharmaceutical drugs can contaminate our water supply. But according to the Food and Drug Administration, you should also avoid disposing of old vitamins and herbal supplements this way, too. Instead, mix old vitamins with coffee grinds and use a nonrecyclable container to dispose of them in the trash. You can also give a few multivitamins to household plants; they'll thrive from the nutritional boost.

33. CORRECT COMPOST

When it comes to composting, organic matter like vegetable and fruit peels are great things to add to your compost bin. But when it comes to citrus peels from fruits like lemons and oranges, it's best to minimize the amount you put into the compost. Citrus oil can be an all-natural pesticide, so adding citrus to your compost can actually be a deterrent for worms to thrive; don't overwhelm your pile with mounds of citrus peels. You can also make a citrus "slurry" with water and leftover lemon in a blender; just pour it into the compost, knowing that the slurry will biodegrade and break down quickly.

34. SAFELY MICROWAVE

If you choose to reheat leftovers in the microwave, opt for microwave-safe reusable containers made out of glass or ceramic. Even plastic containers that are labeled "microwave safe" does not mean they are healthy for you; it only means they can withstand higher temperatures before they soften and change their shape. Plastic containers can still leach chemicals into food and microscopic scratches in plastic containers can also harbor germs and bacteria over time.

35. PRETTY POISONOUS

Who knew that some flowers are more than just beautiful to look at but are useful to help maintain the natural organic health of your garden? Plant lots of chrysanthemum flowers in your garden because it contains a natural chemical called "pyrethin," which is toxic to insects. These beautiful flowers are easy to grow and come in a wide variety of colors, so you can mix them in between vegetables and other plants that are normally a treat for ravenous insects. If you have a problem with insects like Japanese beetles attacking your plants, just mixing in chrysanthemums can do the trick to keep them at bay.

36. BRICK BREAKER

For years, there's been an ecotip that simply putting a brick in the water tank of your toilet can help save water. The idea is that the brick displaces water and turns a water-guzzling toilet into a more efficient one. But the reality is that while you do save half a gallon of water per flush using this method, it can ruin your plumbing. Bricks will disintegrate over time, and those particles and chunks will clog up plumbing. If you want to do this classic ecotip, try filling a plastic tub (like for margarine) with water and place it inside. It'll do the job without the disintegrating pieces.

37. MICROFIBER MAINTENANCE

Microfiber towels have gained a tremendous following because they are reusable and do a great job at gripping dirt, germs, and bacteria when you clean around the house. But with anything that literally absorbs toxins, it's important to clean your microfiber towels, too. A simple technique is to run warm water from the tap over them with a few drops of dishwashing soap. Wring out the cloth (until it appears clean) and microwave the damp microfiber towel in the microwave on high for 90 seconds. This will steam-heat any germs away and give you a fresh-smelling towel. Avoid washing them in the washing machine; microscopic fibers can shed and end up in our waterways this way.

38. FANTASTIC FILM

While placing heavy drapes over windows is a surefire way to keep your home cozy during the winter months, it also blocks sunlight from entering your home. An alternative idea that helps insulate and let sunlight in is using stick-on window film. This self-stick product goes directly onto your window and it's absolutely clear. But it provides an extra layer of insulation that reduces heat loss in winter, blocks harmful UV rays, and in the hot summer months, blocks heat. It's inexpensive and easy to install, and it will pay for itself over time.

39. A BRIGHT IDEA

Want to brighten clothes and remove stains without using any harsh chemicals in your washing machine? Grab salt from your pantry and add it to your laundry routine. The natural chloride in salt works as a brightener, protector, and stain remover all in one. Just add a half cup of salt to your laundry (in addition to your detergent) to give it a natural boost. You can also soak stubborn stains or dull fabrics in a salt water solution overnight and then wash as normal. Another alternative is to use hydrogen peroxide, which breaks down in water and uses oxygen to naturally whiten. Just 1 cup of hydrogen peroxide with regular laundry detergent will be enough.

40. CLEAN IT OUT

While one of the easiest ways to "detox" the air inside your home is to open all the windows in the front and back of the house to flush out toxins, you might wonder: what do you do if your home won't allow that, or the weather is bad? The next best thing is to take advantage of in-house ventilation systems in both the kitchen and bathroom. While the vents are designed to remove excess moisture, odor, and particles, they also do a great job at cleaning the air. The vents are designed to suck in contaminated air and vent it outside. Leave them all on for 30 minutes for a quick indoor air refresh and save the money and energy you'd spend on an air purifier!

41. INSTANT GARDENING

If you're a novice at backyard vegetable gardening and your first season was successful, you may want to take advantage of the cooler weather to expand your garden. In multi-season climates, when the leaves change color, you can pile compost and soil right onto grass to naturally prepare it for plantings in spring. Covering grass in autumn with a few inches of organic planting matter will allow the grass to break down. Sure enough, you'll have new raised beds when the snow melts away.

42. SOY WHAT?

If you love burning candles at home, you may be aware that wax alternatives to paraffin, like soy wax, will burn cleaner and release less pollutants into the air. But when shopping for soy wax candles,  let the buyer beware. If a candle is simply marked "soy wax" or "soy blend," that's no guarantee that they are 100 percent soy. In fact, only 51 percent of the candle needs to be soy wax to be called a soy candle. The other 49 percent? It can be any wax, including paraffin. Look for candles marked 100 percent soy wax to be absolutely sure.

43. RENT AND THEN RENOVATE!

Feel like doing a little DIY at home? Instead of buying expensive and rarely used home improvement equipment, consider renting. Major home improvement chains not only sell products, but they also rent them out. You can find things like tillers, trenchers, sod cutters, chainsaws, and blowers that are both the best of their kind and at a fraction of their cost. Renting also lets you try things out before committing to a full purchase. Rent by the day or the week and turn your basic lawn into a professional-looking showcase.

44. DYE IT RIGHT

Have some black T-shirts or jeans that have faded and could use a little re-dying? There's no need to reach for chemical dyes when there's an all-natural solution: coffee. Two cups of very strong, freshly brewed coffee can reinvigorate black garments. All you do is pour the coffee right into the washing machine when the rinse cycle begins (and also be sure you only have black-dyed items in the machine!). The coffee won't stain the machine and it'll naturally dye your clothes back to a deep black. Be sure to hang-dry the items after they've washed.

45. CHECK AGAIN

It can be really frustrating when an appliance like a washing machine, refrigerator, or stove just stops working. Before you head to the store to buy a new one or hire a repairman, look for some simple solutions. Over time, appliances can slowly shift and move, eventually unplugging themselves. Circuit breakers can also be tripped, so check to make sure you don't need to re-set it. And if the flooring has warped or moved (and the appliance isn't even), some appliances will automatically turn themselves off as a safety precaution.

46. A DIRTY BREW

In 2011, the NSF—a public health and safety organization—found that 50 percent of traditional coffee makers had yeast and mold growing inside. Worse, 10 percent had harmful coliform bacteria. The report stated that "coffee reservoirs had higher germ counts than both bathroom door handles and toilet seats." To prevent this, carafes should be cleaned with hot, soapy water every time you use them. And a simple combination of equal parts white vinegar and water brewed through a coffee maker should disinfect all the internal components of germs and bacteria without any chemicals.

47. TEA TIME

Tea lovers know that tea leaves are so absorbent that you should never store them in the spice cabinet. The reason? Strong spices like cinnamon can actually be absorbed into tea leaves, which can change their flavor profile. But because tea leaves are absorbent, they can also be used to deodorize around the house. Sprinkle dry tea leaves all over a rug or carpet and press them into the carpet. Let them sit for as long as possible (at least 15 minutes) and then vacuum them up. The leaves will absorb odors and leave your carpet smelling like absolutely nothing at all.

48. NOODLE ON THIS

Keeping cold air from entering your home in winter is essential to cut back on heating costs and energy usage. One summertime staple—a pool floatation noodle—can be used to help block drafts. For older homes that often have large gaps under their doors, simply cutting open a pool noodle and sliding it underneath can do the trick. It's soft enough to not scratch floors and it's flexible enough to slide back and forth so the door can actually be opened and used. You can cover it with fabric to make it decorative or just use it as is.

49. WEEDED OUT

When you pull mounds of invasive weeds out of your backyard garden, what do you do with them? Instead of composting them—thereby potentially spreading weed seeds—or just throwing them away, the greenest solution is actually to bag them in black plastic trash bags and *then* compost them. Placing the weeds in a black bag and allowing them to bake in the sun is a simple way to kill the seeds by scorching them with hot sunlight. It's called solarizing. After a few days, simply empty the bag right into the compost and you're good to go. Of course, reuse the bag for its original intended purpose: trash.

50. MULTITASKER

A dishwasher appliance can do more than just get your pots, pans, and dishes sparkling clean. These energy- and water-efficient machines can also sanitize naturally using just hot water and detergent. Use the top rack for things like baseball caps, kids' toys, flip-flops, and light fixture covers to get them clean. Even switchplate covers, fan grilles, and vent covers (all covered in dust, dirt, grease, and debris) can go right in. Using the "rinse-only" cycle is the best way for delicate items or to test something to see how it does inside a dishwasher.

51. START UP A HEALTHIER HOME

One of the biggest sources of air toxicity in your home actually comes from a room in your house: your garage. Homes with attached garages can be more prone to air pollution leaking in. A Canadian health study found that homes with attached garages had high levels of benzene (a chemical from gasoline) while homes without garages had little to none. To prevent toxins from entering your home, obviously never start up a car in a closed garage, but also don't start up lawnmowers, motorcycles, and chainsaws, too. And keep the door from the garage to your home closed and make sure the seal is as tight as possible.

52. VENT A LITTLE

One of the easiest things you can do to create a healthy kitchen is to make use of the range hood vent. Ventilation can help remove air pollution from gas burners, fat particles from frying food, and of course, strong odors from whatever you're cooking up. To make the best use of your kitchen vents, try to cook on the back burners of your cooktop. This is where your vents are at their maximum performance. And don't turn off the vents too early; keep them on until the pans you're cooking with are cool to the touch, for maximum air cleaning efficiency.

53. GREEN IS GOOD

Sure, it's great to upgrade your heating and cooling systems at home to be kind to the environment and reduce your utility bills. But did you know those investments can actually improve the resale value of your home, too? According to the trade magazine *Remodeling*, for every $1 in annual energy savings your improvements provide, you earn up to $20 in home value at the time of sale. For a typical size home of around 2,000 square feet, that can be more than $30,000 in added value. The lower the cost to operate a home, the more valuable it becomes to potential buyers.

54. GARDEN PARTY

If you have a problem with rabbits and other small animals digging up freshly planted flower bulbs from your garden, start collecting used plastic and cardboard berry containers right now. Dig a hole in the ground and insert the berry container, place the bulb inside, and cover with dirt. This activity will create a barrier that prevents animals from digging up the bulbs, while giving the flowers room to send roots downward and grow.

55. POWERED UP

When you replace the alkaline batteries in your smoke and fire detectors with fresh batteries, don't toss those old batteries in the trash. Save those batteries and use them for other household items like remote controls, children's toys, and anything else that uses batteries; they are far from dead. Use them up until they have no charge and then properly dispose of them.

56. SOFT SCRUB

If you use dryer sheets in your dryer, listen up: it's time to wash your lint trap. Over time, dryer sheets leave an invisible film over the small mesh fabric on your lint trap. This prevents your dryer from properly collecting lint, which can not only slow down the efficiency of the dryer but also create a potential fire hazard. To prevent this, remove the lint trap, remove the trapped lint, and then wash it with hot, soapy water and scrub with an old toothbrush. Allow it to dry and it'll help extend the life of your dryer. You'll be amazed at how well your dryer works now.

57. H₂KNOW

One of the easiest ways to save water during the summer months is to know exactly when it's time to water your lawn. First, try this simple trick: step on your lawn. According to the Environmental Protection Agency's Watersense program, if the grass bounces back after you step on it, there's no need to water. If it lays flat, then it's time to water. And then, only water early in the morning or late at night when the sun's rays don't evaporate the water.

58. DON'T BUG OUT

Reclaimed wood is all the rage right now in everything from flooring to furniture. It's eco-friendly because it's reusing wood that came from places like barns and railroads, and it looks good, too. But reclaimed can also mean that the wood could be harboring dangerous insects inside. To make sure your new reclaimed wood table is safe to bring inside, ask if it's been heat-treated. This is an alternative to chemically treating the wood and uses high heat to kill off bugs. Often, you'll find a small mark "HT" on the product to indicate this.

59. GROW LOCAL

If their beauty and eco-friendly nature weren't enough, here's another reason to consider growing native flowers in your own backyard: they are very easy to grow. Usually, when planting a new garden, you have to take the time to weed, till, and amend with organic fertilizer to make the soil rich and loamy. But the reality is native flowers—plants that are indigenous to your growing region—are adapted to regular soil and grow even better in it than they do in fluffy soil.

60. TAKE TWO

Take an aspirin and call me in the morning is a phrase we've all heard. But have you given an aspirin to an ailing houseplant? Turns out it can do a world of good for your plants. When plants are stressed, they create something called salicylic acid to help boost their immune system. The active ingredient in aspirin is called "acetylsalicylic acid," a derivative of salicylic acid. So popping a diluted aspirin in water for plants can help them thrive and stay alive!

61. FLOUR POWER

Do you want your stainless steel sink looking brand new? All you need is a little elbow grease and some leftover flour that may have possibly gone bad. Yes, the same flour you use to make biscuits and cookies can be used to buff and shine up your sink. It works because the flour dust gets into the small grooves of the stainless steel and draws up dirt, grime, and grease that basic soap can't reach. The key thing is this: start with a very dry sink, because any residual water will turn flour into glue. Then buff away with flour, rinse, wipe, and voila! Shiny sink.

62. RAISE THE BAR

Ever wonder what you could do to help a bar soap from dissolving so quickly in the shower? Turns out you need to let a fresh bar of soap "cure" for a few weeks before using it. Many bars of soap are made from a liquid mixture that needs to dry out, or cure, in order for it to be denser, harder, and more long lasting. All you have to do is unwrap the soap you have and let it sit somewhere for 6 to 8 weeks. So when you do buy multiple bars of soap, unwrap them right away so you'll have harder soap when you need it.

63. AN INTIMATE AFFAIR

When it comes to shopping "green," it's always a good thing to look for products made from recycled materials. But when it comes to buying toilet paper, you may want to think twice about buying recycled. Recycled content toilet paper is made from paper fibers like old copy paper, junk mail, and magazines that are shredded, pulped, de-inked, and re-processed. But paper receipts—also known as thermal receipts—can sometimes end up in the recycling waste stream. These receipts are coated in the chemical BPA, a known endocrine disrupter, which can then end up in recycled toilet paper, and when used, BPA can end up in your bloodstream. Go for paper made from sustainable sources like bamboo instead.

64. WINE NOT?

When you accidentally spill a glass of red wine on the carpet, there is no reason to toss out the rug or call a professional cleaner. Instead, do what 007 would do: grab a martini. Red wine contains chemicals called anthocyanins, which are responsible for that deep red color. By dousing red wine with something with a much higher alcohol percentage—vodka, in this case—the anthocynins vanish because they dissolve in the vodka. And like magic, the red wine stain disappears.

65. MAKE IT RAIN

The next time the weather brings in a gentle rain-
storm, consider bringing your indoor plants out-
doors. Yes, it's water-efficient because you're taking advantage of free
water, but there is much more than plant hydration here. Rainwater
also helps give your plants a "bath" of sorts, too; dust and debris on
the plant's leaves will be gently rinsed off. And the rainwater helps do
one more thing: it dissolves built-up salts and minerals on the soil of
your plants that come from tap water.

66. A SMARTER FLUSH

A dual-flush toilet is a great way to save water at home because it lets
you decide if you need a full or partial flush. But if you have a perfectly
fine single flush toilet, what do you do to save water? You can convert
your toilet into a dual-flush just by switching out the toilet flapper. For
less than $10, you can add an adjustable flapper that lets you shorten
the chain on the flapper. This means a conventional toilet that wastes
5 to 7 gallons of water can now be made into a water-efficient one that
uses just 2½ gallons.

67. GOOD TIMING

Large appliances are common in most homes, which means they can be a strain on power grids when everyone is using them at the same time. The peak time for energy usage in most communities is between the hours of 4 p.m. and 6 p.m., when you're often charged more for the "juice." So the best time to run your larger appliances is at night or first thing in the morning. Especially in summer, when air conditioning units are at full blast, changing the time you run your air conditioner or other similar appliances can help reduce your energy bill and decrease the likelihood of a blackout in your area.

68. DRAIN-OH!

Do your kitchen or bathroom drains have an unpleasant scent? Instead of dumping chlorine bleach down the drain to neutralize it, pour in regular salt as a nontoxic solution. Sometimes the stink comes from decomposing organic matter, like food scraps, that's stuck on the sides of pipes. The salt helps dislodge the stuck-on waste and acts like a mini-scrubber for your pipes. Just pour about one half to 1 cup of salt down the drain and turn on the hot water tap.

69. HOUSEWARMING GIFT

If you're registering for gifts for a major event like a wedding or a housewarming, consider registering at a landscaping center for plants. Large balled trees, flowering bushes, and other landscaping plants can be expensive. But over time, they'll mature and add beauty to your yard and also help provide habitat for wild animals. Plus, think of your registered gifts as something that will grow with you over time. And don't forget: most nurseries offer a guarantee on plants, so if one or two trees don't make it, they can be replaced free of charge.

70. LUSCIOUS LATHER

Here's another reason to switch from bottled body wash to bar soap: you get more active ingredients when you switch to a bar. When you buy a bottled body wash, the primary ingredient is water. With bar soap, there is very little (if any) water in the bar, which means every ingredient is active and designed to do its job. Also, there is no plastic packaging, it's lighter (so there's less of a carbon footprint to have bars shipped to stores versus bottles), and for you road warriors: it's TSA-friendly, too.

71. POCKET CHANGE

Spare change that accidentally ends up in a load of laundry seems like no big deal, but the reality is that it can cause serious damage. Because washing machines use a centrifugal force to draw water out of wet clothes, it can turn a few pennies, nickels, and dimes into damaging projectiles inside the machine, causing damage to your machine's mechanical components. Make it a habit to check every pocket so every wash is a coin-free one. This one step can help prevent your washing machine from breaking down.

72. GO PAPER TOWEL-LESS

Aside from being wasteful, paper towels can also harbor germs. A study at Laval University in Quebec City showed that bacteria can thrive even on unused towels! The pulping process at factories that make towels can often be contaminated themselves, spreading germs like the Bacillus spore right onto the towel. While no illness has been linked to paper towels, why go with single-use towels when reusable ones are just fine?

73. COLD SHOWER

This isn't a groundbreaking tip, but it's one worth repeating. When washing your clothes, opt to use the cold water setting whenever possible. The reason is simple: as much as 85 percent of the energy used to wash clothing is from heating water! By choosing the cold water setting, you're significantly reducing your energy usage in that load of laundry. Plus, cold water works well with modern detergents and helps reduce wear and tear on clothes, too.

74. BB-CLUES

As temperatures dip, one pricey outdoor investment that should be brought indoors is the backyard grill. Snow and ice can cause significant damage and make them unusable when warmer months come back around. The best place to store them is in the garage or basement. When storing any gas grill, you should have the tank valve closed and the propane tank removed. And even if it's brought indoors, be sure to scrub the insides clean. Any residual food waste charred inside can be tempting for wild critters.

75. ICE, ICE, BABY

Icicles on the side of the home may look pretty, but they really can cause significant water damage to your home when things begin to thaw out. The main culprit of what are called "ice dams" on the edges of your house are clogged gutters. Make sure your gutters are clear. This ensures that water can freely flow and won't freeze up during the winter months. This one thing can help you save thousands of dollars in repairs.

76. SOCK IT TO ME

It's inevitable: you lose a sock. So what do you do with the stray single sock that remains? Don't toss it when you can reuse it around the house. One simple solution is to fill a sock with cedar shavings and tie

a knot at the end to prevent the shavings from spilling out. Because socks are porous, the cedar scent will permeate the air inside a closet and keep moths at bay. Or, to keep your car windows from fogging up, fill a sock with kitty liter and tie a knot at the end. Place it by the window and it'll absorb excess moisture, keeping your car windshield perfectly clear.

77. ROOM REDO

Smart decorating can help improve the natural flow of a home and make use of every inch of space. But decorating can also help you keep your home warmer during the winter months. Older homes often have no sidewall insulation, which can absorb cold air from outdoors and add chill inside a home. To insulate them, you can place bookshelves or other heavy furniture against the wall to block cold air. Also, hanging decorative quilts can look good and insulate, too.

78. KEEP IT CLEAN

While disposable razors may not be an environmentally friendly choice, if you do use them, there is one thing you can do to help lengthen the lives of the blades. After each shave, simply rinse and dip the blades in a little isopropyl rubbing alcohol. This does two things: It helps dry out the razor blades, which means they won't rust and will stay sharp. And it helps sanitize the blades, which means you won't be introducing acne-inducing bacteria onto your face with each shave. You can also dip nail clippers and tweezers in alcohol to keep them clean.

79. GREEN JUICE

Don't have room to compost? Even if you have a very small yard, you can still help divert organic matter from going into the landfill. Just put small pieces of vegetable and fruit peels and skins into a blender and puree with water until it becomes a liquid, slushy mixture. Then dig a small hole in the yard, pour the nutrient-dense mixture into the hole, and cover with soil. It'll deliver all the benefits of compost to plants without attracting pests, too.

80. ZERO IS YOUR HERO

If you're taking on a DIY painting project in your home, you may think buying a "low-VOC" (which is short for volatile organic compounds) paint is the healthiest and greenest option out there. But the reality is almost all household paints are technically "low" VOC. What you do want to look for are paints marked "zero" VOC, which means it has no odor in its untinted form. And then use a brand where the tints are zero- to low-VOC to make sure your final color choice is as green as it can be.

81. OLD ISN'T NEW

Enamelware serving pieces and cookware were common in the late nineteenth and early twentieth centuries, so you might find them at flea markets, antiques stores, or thrift shops. But are these older enamelware dishes safe to use now for serving food and cooking? Most likely not. Back in the day, there was little regulation on what manufacturers could use to make enamelware, so often vintage pieces have additives like lead and cadmium. If you do find and purchase old enamelware, use it for display or decorative use only.

82. CHILL OUT

Take a look inside your freezer: is it full or half empty? If it's the latter, go reuse a freezer bag or two and fill it with ice. When you have bags of ice cubes in the freezer, it takes up space and helps keep the overall freezer temperature down. The cooler the freezer, the less energy it uses to keep itself at the appropriate temperature. Even filling some old ice cream containers with water and letting them freeze into blocks of ice can go a long way toward improving your freezer's efficiency.

83. STOP SOAKING

Many of us soak our cookware in water for several hours or overnight to loosen baked-on food to make cleanup easier. While that does work, it also can warp the pan over time, making it defective and difficult to use. To protect your cookware investment, allow your pan to cool to room temperature and then immerse into water for several minutes. That should be enough soaking time to make cleanup easier without risking any damage to the pan.

84. REPURPOSE YOUR PLANTS

Got a dead houseplant? It can be so easy to simply pick up the whole thing and toss it into the trash, but its final destination shouldn't be a landfill where it can't properly decompose. Instead, spread the dead plant and soil onto your lawn and simply run your lawnmower over it. It'll help break up all the organic matter into smaller pieces and it'll decompose and help contribute to healthier soil and a better lawn.

85. HOW COOL

Did you know your water heater can also take a vacation? Maybe not to a faraway destination, but it can be set to use less energy when you place it on "vacation" or "away" mode. In some homes, a water heater can make up as much as 25 percent of your home's overall energy usage. And as always, raise or lower your thermostat depending on the season; according to the Department of Energy, you should set it to 85 degrees in summer and 50 degrees during colder months.

86. POWDER POWER

Did you know liquid laundry detergents have a shelf life? The ingredients in liquid laundry detergent—like whitening agents—break down over time and become less effective at getting your clothes clean. Do this one thing: switch to powdered laundry detergents, which last longer and are more shelf stable. If you've stopped using powdered detergents because they cake up and clog your washing machine, try dissolving it in hot water ahead of time. Simply fill a pitcher with hot tap water and add the recommended amount of powdered detergent. Stir, dissolve, and pour into your washing machine. All the ecobenefits of powder and the convenience of liquid.

87. SLEEP SMARTER

When it's time to replace your mattress, you might wonder what you should do with your old one. If it's in decent shape, you should try to find a friend or family member who would be willing (and needing) the bed, as most nonprofits do not accept old beds. But if it's in bad shape and ready to be disposed of, the good news is that it is recyclable. Approximately 90 percent of the materials used to make a conventional mattress can be recycled. To find a recycler near you, just visit the website byebyemattress.com and enter your zip code to find local facilities.

88. UP ON THE ROOFTOP

Take a moment to examine your roof to look for what's called "popped nails." These are nails that were used to secure roofing shingles that have done just that: popped up. Over time—whether it's humidity, environmental concerns, or just warping—a few nails can come loose and rise up. Why is this important to address now? Because a popped nail is a small hole where water can seep in and create damage. And if you live in an area prone to heavy storms, this also could be a part of the roof that "lifts" during a storm, creating even more damage. If you see several popped nails, have a professional fix them to save yourself any long-term damage and wasted materials.

89. COLOR CORRECTING

Did you know one of the top reasons household paint is "wasted" is because the color we chose is the wrong shade? It can be hard to choose the perfect shade from myriad paint chips, and often when we pick something we like, it appears to be too bright, too dark, or just wrong on our walls. To help avoid this financial and material waste, look to other homes and spaces for color inspiration. When you find a wall color you like, you can use a number of apps to immediately color-match it on your phone. Then order that exact shade, so you have the perfect color in your soon-to-be-perfect home.

90. MARKER REVIVAL

Got a dried-out marker that just won't work when you try to bring ink to paper? Don't toss it in the trash. Whatever the reason is for the dried-out tip (maybe you left the cap off overnight?), it can be resuscitated. All you have to do is place the tip of the marker in a small amount of rubbing alcohol and let it soak for 15 minutes. The rubbing alcohol will self-lubricate the inside of the marker and help unblock any dried-out areas. Give it a try on a piece of scrap paper and your pen will be as good as new.

91. LIGHTER LOAD

With lots of laundry to do, it might seem like an economical and time-saving idea to slightly overload the washing machine. The problem with this cleaning tactic is that the weight of the excess wet clothing could wear out the machine's internal drum and start to decrease the machine's overall cleaning efficiency. The reality is that when clothing doesn't have room to be agitated and washed, it doesn't come out clean. And redoing your laundry more often just adds up to more water and energy waste.

92. BRIGHT IDEA

One of the tricks of interior decorators to make a space feel more special is to install dimmer switches so you can control the amount of light a fixture shines. But does a dimmer light also mean energy savings? And an extra bonus: it turns out a dimmer switch can also mean more energy savings. It works because light dimmers reduce the flow of electricity to a lighting fixture, which means the bulbs work at lower power outputs. It also means the light bulbs will last longer because there's less wear and tear on them, too.

93. DIRTY TRUTH

Can you reuse old soil from potted plants? The answer is no, unless you know absolutely for sure that the soil is free of any disease. Given that it can be impossible to tell, the best way to reuse potting soil is to sprinkle it in the yard, where the sun will have a chance to "bake" the soil (killing any disease) and eventually blend right into the ground. And those plastic pots that once held your houseplants? Reuse them or bring them to a big-box retailer to be recycled free of charge.

94. ASHES TO ASHES

If you're warming up by the outdoor fire pit, do this: save the ashes. One cord of wood can produce about 50 pounds of ashes, and these ashes have a number of beneficial uses around your property. If you grow tomatoes, sprinkle and rake ashes into the soil; they love the natural calcium in wood ashes and will thrive. You can also spread the ashes to make a border around the garden; it acts as a natural barrier to damaging slugs and other pests.

95. POWER DOWN

Leaving your home for several long weeks or even months means you should take steps to reduce waste while you're away. This is a good time to unplug energy hogs like refrigerators and freezers; just be sure they are empty and leave the doors open so they dry out completely. Turn off the main water supply; it may not save you money, but it'll give you peace of mind there won't be a plumbing break. Turn off the electric water heater tank at the main breaker switch; there's no point in keeping water hot for weeks at a time if it's not being used. And switch off modems, cable boxes, and small kitchen appliances by unplugging them from the electric sockets.

96. GO FOR COLD

Turns out washing your clothes in cold water does more than save energy and money on your utility bill: it also preserves your clothes. The fibers of your clothing last longer in cold water and actually deteriorate when washed in hot water. The only time you really need to wash in hot water is if you need to remove stubborn stains that are oil-based or to disinfect things like hand towels and bedding. Otherwise, 9 out of 10 washes on average should be done in cold water. You'll save money on your electric bill and help extend the life of your clothes, too.

97. H₂ UH OH

An outdoor leak can be very hard to detect, because drips will often simply go into the ground and not leave any sign that there's a problem. To see if your outdoor faucets are leaking, wrap a balloon around the opening of the faucet and hold it in place with a tight rubber band or zip tie. Then come back a few days later. If it's full  of water, you've got a leak and will need to fix it to avoid wasting any more water.

98. HOT STUFF

If you're choosing blinds for your windows and live in a hot climate, avoid metal blinds. During the day, the sun's rays can heat up the metal blinds and essentially turn them into a hanging radiator in your home. The better solution is to look for fabric blinds, like cellular shades, or bamboo to block out the light and help keep your thermostat down. Some blinds are also eligible for federal tax-saving credits as part of the Energy Efficient Home Improvement Credit, so be sure to ask when purchasing to see if they're eligible.

99. GREENER CLEAN

When it's time to empty your vacuum's collection bin, you might wonder: is it compostable? Depends. If you have nylon carpet or rugs at home, then most likely these are not good candidates for composting. The reason is that small fibers of synthetic material will end up in the collection of dust, dirt, and debris. If your vacuum was used over hardwood, ceramic, and natural fiber rugs, then it could be composted. Just take a quick look and make sure there are no obvious signs of synthetic materials before composting.

100. PRINTER PROBLEMS

Do you use a laser printer in your home office? Turns out there's a possibility that every time you print out a page, you might be inhaling toxic ultrafine particles. Scientists at the Queensland University of Technology studied the particle emissions of 62 common printers. Around 40 percent emitted particles, and among those, 27 percent emitted a high level. Cardiovascular problems have been linked to ultrafine particles, including those from printers. If you do use a laser printer, try to keep it away from where you work or use it in a well-ventilated area.

101. SAY NO TO INSECTICIDES

Do you use mothballs to keep your sweaters and knits safe from being destroyed by moths and their larvae? Simply put: don't. Turns out mothballs are made entirely from a chemical called naphthalene, which basically means they slowly turn from a solid "ball" into a chemical vapor. In other words, if you can smell mothballs, you're inhaling the chemical insecticide. Try natural repellants like cedar chips or create a sachet with dried herbs like rosemary, thyme, and bay leaves.

102. SEED STARTER

When it's time to replace an old kitchen sponge, don't toss it away. An old sponge is the perfect growing medium to use as a seed starter for flowers and vegetables. It's easy: Just place seeds inside the nooks and natural holes of the sponge (or make small slices with the tip of a knife) and mist the sponge well with water. Place it in a dish with a little more water and be sure to keep it moist. In days, you'll see the seeds sprout. When the seedlings are strong enough, you can transplant them into a growing medium or just trim the sponge and plant the seedlings with the remaining sponge material still attached.

103. PILLOW TALK

Many sleep experts recommend replacing your bed pillows around every 2 years. The reason is your pillows absorb a lot over many nights of sleep including body oil, sweat, and dead skin cells. If you can't recall when you bought your pillows, do this simple test instead: fold your pillow in half. If it doesn't bounce back right away or—worse—stays folded in half, it's time to replace that pillow. Also, invest in a pillow cover to create an extra barrier to help provide an even healthier sleep.

104. A POP-ULAR IDEA

A little party at your home may mean you have some undrunk soda pop in cans and glasses at the end of the festivities. Don't toss it down the drain when it can be used to get your pots and pans gleaming. Just pour the leftover soda into your dirty cookware and let it simmer on very low heat for about for 30 to 45 minutes. Soda—the dark kind like Coke and Pepsi—is highly acidic and does wonders to eat away at stubborn messes.

105. RAZOR SHARP

Did you know buying a pre-loved used kitchen knife from a resell site or flea market can save as much as 90 percent on energy costs needed to make a new knife? To sanitize a used knife, you can do it in seconds at home. If the knife does not have a plastic handle, place the knife in boiling water for 30 seconds. Turn off the heat and let the knife sit in the hot water and slowly pour out the boiling water; allow the knife to cool to room temperature. If the knife has a plastic handle, fill a pot with the hottest water that comes out of the tap and let the knife soak for 30 seconds. Remove with tongs and scrub with an old toothbrush with soap and water.

106. TERRIFIC TOWELS

Have stinky bath towels? It's not because you're not washing them enough. You're actually washing them too much. Because bath towels are so absorbent, when you use regular laundry detergent on them it actually absorbs the soap particles into the fibers of the towel. That buildup over time gives towels a musty, mildew smell that only gets worse the more you wash them using laundry detergent. Instead, wash all your towels with just a few cups of white vinegar and hot water alone. It will rinse the soap buildup away and your towels will be like new.

107. DRY CLEAN NEVER

There's no need for chemical dry cleaning when wool sweaters can be safely and easily washed at home, right? You can do a bunch of sweaters at the same time, too. All you need to do is fill a bathtub with lukewarm water and add gentle laundry detergent. Soak the sweaters for 10 minutes in the soapy water and drain. Refill with water to rinse them and then rinse them by hand in cold water. Just lay the sweaters on clean towels to blot out the excess and let them lay flat until dry.

108. CURTAINS UP

Shower curtain liners can get dirty quickly from soap scum, mildew, and hard water. To extend the life of your shower curtain, try pretreating it in your washing machine. It's a process that involves running it in warm water through the rinse cycle of your machine. Instead of detergent, use some white vinegar to treat it. This creates a scant coating on the shower curtain that prevents soap scum and stains from attaching to the shower curtain. And don't forget: wash your shower curtain periodically in the washing machine.

109. COOL IDEA

The Natural Resources Defense Council says a typical refrigerator uses 10 to 15 percent of an entire household's energy bill each month. That's a lot. While unplugging a fridge when you go away is the *most* efficient, it really isn't realistic. Do the next best thing: raise the temperature of your refrigerator from 38 to 42 degrees. It's cold enough to keep food preserved but helps make your appliance much more energy-efficient when you're away.

110. GREAT GARDEN

Smart planning for your flower beds around the house can lead to significant water and time savings when caring for your gorgeous flowers. According to *National Geographic*, you can consider "companion planting" by grouping certain plants together to help them mutually grow. By planting taller, sun-loving plants in the back next to shorter, shade-loving plants in front, you help the plants thrive. The taller plants block the sun's rays and also help reduce evaporation of water in the shorter plants.

111. A HOT IDEA

Air fryers are all the rage right now, and in addition to making your food extra crispy, another bonus to their use is that they're energy-efficient. Air fryers use hot air with very little oil to cook whatever you're crisping up, and because they are significantly smaller than an oven, they also take very little time to heat up from room temperature to literally hundreds of degrees. In fact, in the time it can take to preheat an oven, an air fryer can cook an entire dinner. And unlike deep frying, there's no waste oil to dispose of when you're finished.

112. A GOOD TRIM

If you see a houseplant with yellowing leaves, one of the most important things you should do to keep your plants healthy and happy is trim them off. The reality is that yellow or almost dead leaves won't revive and turn green again, so it's better to help the plant remove them so they can dedicate all their energy to regenerating new leaves. When you are done pruning, be sure to wipe the blades with rubbing alcohol. This will disinfect the blades so you don't transfer any diseases to other plants.

113. NUTTY IDEA

Ever wonder what to do with the shells of nuts from walnuts, pecans, and pistachios? Scatter them as beneficial mulch in the garden. If there is any residual salt on the shells, that will help deter slugs from attacking your plants. One other idea is to use them for indoor houseplants, too. Line the bottom of a planter with shells and fill with soil. It will help provide draining for the plant and will decompose down into beneficial mulch for your houseplant over time. If there is residual salt on the shells, simply soak them in water first to remove any salt.

114. ODORS BE GONE

Here's a chemical-free way to make a deodorizing fabric refresher with just two ingredients! Mix equal parts vodka and water into a spray bottle and use it to deodorize and freshen up the inside of shoes, jackets, and clothing you haven't quite gotten around to washing. It can also help freshen odors that might be in upholstered furniture, curtains, and even inside your car. Vodka kills the germs that cause odor and the water helps dilute it enough so it's not too strong on fabrics.

115. A LUCKY LAWN

Do you have restrictions where you live on the amount of water you can use to water your lawn and garden? Turns out the traditional turf uses a lot of water and fertilizer to look lush and green. It might be a good time to consider a greener alternative: clover. Clover plants are easy to grow and can cover just like grass, but their deep roots mean they need less water to thrive and are drought-resistant. Doesn't a lawn of four-leaf (lucky) clovers sound nice?

116. LINE DRY

Did you know that, according to the Natural Resources Defense Council, Americans spend over $9 billion a year on electricity simply to dry clothes? While hanging all our laundry to air dry isn't probably realistic for most of us, we can make an effort to air dry some items in our home. Think about air drying items that tend to shrink, like sweaters and T-shirts or towels, that can take a long time to dry in the dryer. Every little bit of clothing counts.

117. SLOW AND STEADY

Dishwashers are designed to be as water- and energy-efficient as possible, and they are a greener choice than washing by hand. It may seem that opting for a "quick" or "1-hour mode" for your dishwasher would save energy, but it's actually the opposite. Just like driving a car more slowly saves on fuel, energy efficiency for your dishwasher is gained by extending cycle time, which reduces both electricity and water usage. A quick wash means more resources have to be used to gain the same performance in your machine.

118. LINE COOK

If there's a lot of sautéing, frying, and cooking going on in your kitchen, make sure your stove is working and venting properly. A gas range gives off a small amount of carbon monoxide (CO), which is perfectly normal and won't get you sick. But too much CO and you could be

in trouble. Take a look at the flames on your cooktop: are they yellow-tipped flames? That means the CO levels are too high and the burners need to be fixed. And if you have an exhaust fan, use it: it removes excess CO, particulates, and smoke. Be sure the exhaust fan filters are clean and also properly installed.

119. A CLEAN CLIP

One of the greenest things you can do when taking care of your lawn is to leave the grass clippings in your yard instead of stuffing them into trash bags. But it's also important to make sure those clippings (and leaves and other organic yard debris) stay in your yard and not on hard surfaces like your driveway and sidewalks. The reason? When it rains, this debris can end up in storm drains and waterways, causing algae blooms. It's better that they decompose naturally in your yard.

120. CARPET COLLECTION

If you're ripping out old wall-to-wall carpet, it's worth the effort to find a recycling facility to take it instead of sending it to a landfill. The good news is that carpet and carpet padding are recyclable, and it's made into a plastic resin that's used to make a wide range of home and automotive products. To find a recycler, just visit carpetrecovery.org and locate a recycler on the "collector finder map." Because carpet recycling isn't something you'll likely do on a regular basis, doing this one-time extra step can go a long way to help reduce landfill waste.

121. CAST AWAY

Cast iron is an excellent choice to cook with because it is incredibly durable, naturally nonstick, and free of any questionable chemicals like PTFE and PFOA found in many nonstick pans today. If you're in the market for a cast-iron skillet, however, avoid the temptation to buy a "preseasoned" one. Preseasoned means the pan has been pre-sprayed with a layer of fat at the factory. Because the source of fat is not required to be on the label, those with peanut allergies could be affected by preseasoned pans. Instead, look for raw iron pans and season them yourself, using your own oils, so you know exactly what's in the pan when you cook with it.

122. REPAIRMAN CALLING

When a major appliance goes bust, many people immediately go to the store and buy a new one. But with new high-tech appliances costing up to thousands of dollars, a simple $75 to $100 repair bill to fix a refrigerator, dishwasher, or washer/dryer can not only bring it back to perfect working order but also save you money. In general, the life cycle of major appliances like a fridge, freezer, range, dishwasher, washer, and dryer is between 10 and 15 years, and for a window box air conditioner, about 7 years. If your appliance's life falls within those years, consider repair before replacement.

123. ODOR EATER

If you get a shipment and it's full of Styrofoam packing peanuts, reuse and recycle them. Yes, styrofoam packing peanuts can easily be recycled for shipping purposes or they can be dropped off at local mail-and ship-for-you stores to be reused. But did you know they can also help deodorize a refrigerator or musky drawer? If you want to get rid of a smell, fill a drawer or the compartments inside a refrigerator with packing peanuts. Let them sit overnight (or 24 hours for maximum effect) to absorb odors. Remove and recycle the packing peanuts as you normally would. It really works!

124. BAD SCENT

While it may seem all-natural, burning incense in your home can equal the polluting effects of smoking cigarettes. Incense has the chemical benzene (also found in cigarettes), and this carcinogenic is released in the air when you burn it. Instead, try oil burners to get fragrant scents in the air. These "burners" warm up scented oil using a candle and gently waft the scent without releasing any smoke in the air.

125. PERFECT PILLOW

Here's a simple way to reuse old pillowcases: store your sweaters inside them! The cases will allow the sweaters to breathe while protecting them from the elements and dust. You also can protect clothing that you hang—like jackets and shirts—by using old pillowcases. Simply cut a hole in the middle of the closed side and drape it over the hanging clothing to cover and protect your garment. Your local thrift store is a great place to find pillowcases if you want to protect a whole closet's worth of clothing.

126. CLEAN SWEEP

Disposable wet mops have become popular for their convenience and ease of cleaning. But the throwaway pads can be wasteful and expensive, too. Save the mop and skip buying new pads by saving old T-shirts and use them instead. Simply cut the T-shirts in half and wrap them around the head of the mop. Spray a natural cleaner on the floor and mop away. The T-shirts are machine-washable and can be used over and over to keep your floors sparkling clean.

127. EXTRA, EXTRA

Nearly 16 million printed newspapers are sold every week in the United States, which means many homes have stacks of newsprint. Yes, it's recyclable, but it's also a great material to use around the house. Stuff shoes with newspaper to deodorize them; the absorbent paper soaks up odors and excess moisture. Cover an area of the yard that has weeds with newspaper; it'll block out the sun and slowly kill them (plus the paper will break down into beneficial mulch for the yard). And wrap a present with newspaper for a last-minute gift wrapping hack.

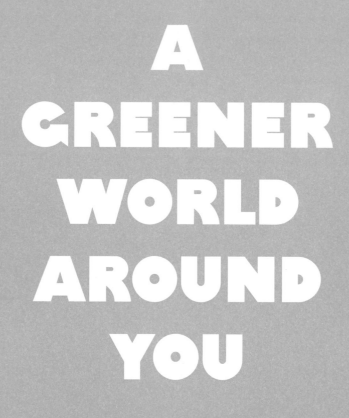

CHAPTER 2

A GREENER WORLD AROUND YOU

When we venture out of our homes, what we do has a direct impact on others and on the environment we move through. We make connections. But the fact is that the trains, planes, and automobiles we rely on pose some of the biggest roadblocks to creating a healthier environment. Even our digital and electronic connections come with an environmental cost. From regular commutes to the office and shuttling kids to errands and even the way we recycle our home products back into the world, extracurricular activities can all add up. It's our everyday choices that may seem meaningless, but they can actually be meaningful if done with the planet in mind.

I'd be the last person to suggest you avoid getting out into the world—I love to travel and connect with people—but I'm the first one to let you know that a few minor shifts in how you do it will move us all in a better direction.

128. POP IT

Another reason to skip balloons for birthday parties and other celebrations: there is a helium shortage. It's expected that helium gas will be gone by the year 2030 if used at current levels. So, why is this important? Because helium gas is used for more than just balloons: in science (especially the science of cryogenics), helium gas is used in high-energy accelerators, arc welding, and silicon wafer manufacturing (the chips that help power your cars and phones). The very high melting and boiling points of helium also make it a unique natural element for scientific research. As the US government begins to create helium reserves to save the precious gas, the easiest way for consumers to help is to simply say no to helium-filled balloons.

Here's another reason to not get balloons for your next occasion: they can cause power outages. According to the nonprofit Energy Education Council, metallic balloons are a special type of nylon with a thin external metal coating. When these metallic balloons are accidentally released into the air, they can get caught in power lines. And it's this thin metal coating that can cause power outages and even fires.

129. PHONE HACK

Did you know one of the fastest ways to ruin a smart phone comes from Mother Nature? When your phone is exposed to the hot rays of the sun too long, it can overheat and not only degrade the performance of the battery but melt the internal components, potentially ruining the phone for good. The easiest way to avoid this is to keep the phone out of the sun and especially to never leave a phone inside a hot car (including the glove box, which still gets very hot). And when charging up a phone on a hot day, take off the protective case before charging; the case can hold on to heat and cause the phone to overheat, too.

130. SPARK JOY

Do you have a junk or office desk drawer just overflowing with random cords and cables for electronics, phones, and other devices? If you're unsure what goes with what, you can declutter and recycle those cords. Many national electronics retailers will happily take those cords for free recycling at no charge to you. So what's in it for them? They can recycle the copper used inside the cords! It's a win-win: you get to clean up and also keep electronic waste out of the landfill.

131. LEAVE THE SPARE

If you only drive locally, there's no need to have a spare tire in your car (especially if you don't know how to replace one). A spare tire weighs about 39 pounds, which reduces your car's efficiency by 1 percent. That may not sound like a lot, but it's about an extra $50 in gas, money you could be saving, and gas you could be emitting less of! Instead of the spare, keep a can of "Fix a Flat" on hand, which can temporarily inflate a flat tire so you can drive to a repair shop and get it fixed. When you do go on long-distance trips or travel, do place the spare tire back in the car so you're prepared for wherever your travels may take you.

132. FREQUENT FLIER

Is there really an ecological difference in the type of airline you fly on? While plane travel may not be the most fuel-efficient way to travel, sometimes it's just unavoidable and your choice of airline *can* make an impact. When choosing between aisle or window, make sure you also factor in the choice for all-coach airlines like Jet Blue and Southwest. Given that first-class seats take up more room for fewer passengers, airlines that offer all-coach seating maximize space and increase the plane's per-passenger capacity. In the long run, the total carbon emissions per passenger is less than planes with first-class seating sections.

133. SKIP THE SPAM

Did you know that spam e-mail can also lead to the waste of natural resources? According to internet security firm McAfee, about 62 *trillion* spam emails are sent annually and they use up enough electricity to power up more than 2.4 million homes. All the energy used to power up computers and smart phones—including the time wasted from deleting unwanted emails—adds up. One way to prevent this is to install spam filter software to stop it from clogging your inbox.

134. SELF AUDIT

One way to find out if your car is in need of servicing is to simply do a self gas audit on your vehicle. The next time you fill up on gas, take a note of your mileage. Then, the next time you fill up, note the new mileage. The third time you fill up, compare the mileage used from the first and second fill-ups on gas. If there is a decent disparity between the mileages, there is a chance your car needs servicing. You can also check your car's owner manual to see what they state as your vehicle's average miles per gallon. Anything that is substantially off is an indicator that something needs to be tuned up to make your car run as efficiently as possible.

135. LIGHT FLIGHT

It's no surprise that flying on a plane isn't the most eco-friendly way to travel, but sometimes it's the *only* way to get where you need to go. One way to help reduce your carbon footprint when you fly is to simply pack less. The more weight from over-packed suitcases on the plane, the more fuel it needs to fly. If every passenger on a domestic flight simply packed 5 pounds less stuff, that would save over 60 million gallons of fuel every year. Take out one pair of shoes, a few books, and a pair of jeans, and voila! Five pounds gone.

136. LEAVE IT TO THE PROS

It's a DIY world, but here's one task you should leave to the professionals: changing your car's motor oil. If you do it yourself and have a spill, the used oil can contaminate up to one million gallons of fresh water. The reason is that motor oil is insoluble, has heavy metals in it, and is very slow to biodegrade. Even trace amounts in water (undetectable to the eye) are enough to make it unsafe. By bringing your car to a trained professional, you know your car will get the new motor oil it needs to function properly, and every last drop of used oil will get recycled and refined.

137. TRICKY RECYCLING

When it comes to recycling your cans, bottles, and boxes at home, the most commonly recycled plastics are the ones marked with a #1 or #2 mark on the bottom. But beware: there are certain #1 marked plastics—specifically, things like black plastic microwavable trays—that are most likely not recyclable. You might be wondering why they're labeled incorrectly, but they're really not: plastics like these trays are usually marked #1s, not just #1. The #1s mark is reserved for a different grade of plastic resin that is harder to recycle and, if commingled with other plastics, could contaminate a load of recyclables. When in doubt, toss plastics marked #1s into the trash.

138. LET IT GO

If you have a cargo unit on the roof of your car, you may want to rethink how you use it. While it may be helpful for carrying camping gear for a summer road trip, it only wastes gas when you're not actually using it. Cars are designed to be as aerodynamic as possible, and a cargo unit on the roof decreases your car's efficiency significantly. Your overall fuel efficiency can decrease as much as 25 percent when you drive around with the unit on the roof. If you must have a cargo box and are buying a new one, consider a rear-mounted one, which only decreases your car's efficiency around 5 percent. Or, if you already have a roof-mounted unit, make sure you remove it when it's not full of gear, so your day-to-day driving is as efficient as possible.

139. BATTERY POWERED

The nonprofit program Call2Recycle has been collecting old rechargeable batteries—the types found in cordless products, cell phones, and kids' toys—for over 20 years with over 100 million pounds of rechargeable batteries collected and recycled. But did you know you can also toss your dead electric toothbrush in their recycling bins? Personal care products that have an integrated rechargeable battery can be recycled easily: You don't need to remove the battery. Just toss the whole electric toothbrush in the box and it will get recycled. The metals, plastics, and other parts will be sorted and made into new products. Learn more at call2recycle.org.

140. GOLD RUSH

Strange but true: old dentures contain valuable gold and silver inside them that can be salvaged, recycled, and make you some money. There are two ways you can recycle dentures. Ask a reputable jeweler who buys gold to see if they can help phish out the metal. Or try the website crownmen.com, which specializes in turning dental waste into cold hard cash.

141. COMPUTER PROCESSING

Is your computer running slowly? It may not be the result of viruses or a lack of memory on the hard drive. It could actually be the surge protector that your computer is plugged into. A surge protector is a wise investment to help prevent damage to your pricey electronics; they prohibit electrical surges from harming them. But just like any electrical products, surge protectors also wear down over time. An old surge protector can deliver inadequate power to your computer. So, to test it, plug your computer into a wall socket and see if it speeds up or acts as good as new. If so, it's time to get a new surge protector (and recycle the old one for free at Best Buy).

142. POP GOES THE RECYCLER

What to do with all the packaging that comes with online orders? When it comes to both plastic bubble wrap and plastic air pillows (usually used to cushion your order in the box), they can be easily recycled. Find a plastic shopping bag recycling bin (many supermarkets have them), and deposit them into that recycling bin. Plastic packaging is made from the same kind of plastic as the shopping bags and will be recycled into new plastic products. Just do one thing before putting them in: pop the bubbles, so they don't fill up all the room in the recycling bin.

143. BOOK SMART

Have you ever wondered if you can recycle old books? Of course, you can always donate gently used books to a used bookstore, Goodwill, or the Salvation Army. But if you have damaged books that bookstores won't carry, you might be able to recycle them. It all depends on the type of book and if you're willing to take one extra step to make them recyclable. For paperback books, you can toss them in standard paper recycling bins, given that the whole book is recyclable paper (just be sure to remove any plastic coverings. But when it comes to hardcover books, you'll need to rip off the cover and spine due to the thick composite and glues used to bind the cover. That cover can be tossed into the trash and all the interior pages can easily be recycled.

144. PACK IT UP

If you love to hike or camp in the Great Outdoors, healthy snacks like apples, bananas, and oranges are easy to pack and carry to fuel your workout. But when you get down to the core or peels of these items, it may seem harmless to chuck the fully biodegradable waste right into the woods, right? The reality is, it's not that easy for the items to biodegrade all on their own. Apple cores can take 8 weeks to break down and the peels can take up to 2 full years. They don't break down like they do in a compost because there aren't any natural microorganisms to turn them into beneficial mulch. Whenever you're camping, always remember to pack in and pack out: carry out any trash you brought with you.

145. DON'T FAN THE FUMES

If you've ever found the smell of gas annoying while at the filling station, you're not wrong to be irritated: it's not just obnoxious, it could be toxic. The fumes you smell are likely benzene and toluene fumes, which can lead to overall health problems. When pumping gas, the proper way to fill up is to insert the nozzle into your gas tank and use something called the "hold-open latch" that pumps gas continuously without needing to hold the nozzle. Stand a few feet away to avoid the fumes and be sure to not top off the tank, which can release additional fumes into the atmosphere.

146. AT THE CAR WASH

When it's time to wash your car, a professional car wash is the greenest choice. The Environmental Protection Agency says the automated car wash not only is the most water- and energy-efficient method, but it also properly disposes of and recycles wastewater. But if you want to wash your car at home, do it on gravel or grass; runoff water on pavement is unfiltered water and can pollute waterways. Allowing wastewater to filter through just dirt and gravel can minimize pollution.

147. SPARK IT UP

If your car has driven just about over 30,000 miles, it's time to replace the spark plugs. Over time, spark plugs can become covered in carbon deposits, which makes them work harder and decreases your car's overall fuel efficiency. When your car misfires (when the engine stops for a brief second and keeps on going), it's a sure sign your spark plugs need replacing. Misfires increase exhaust emissions and that can completely impact your overall MPGs for your car, too.

148. UNTIL NEXT SUMMER

The active ingredients in sunscreen needs to be protected from harsh, hot, and bright elements (just like your skin does). Avoid storing bottles of sunscreen in your car, in your golf bag, or in your beach bag when not in use. Long-term exposure to heat and sun can turn them from skin protectors to simple moisturizers in no time flat. Instead, when you're not having fun in the sun, keep them in the fridge. The cool, dark environment preserves them until the next time you have some fun in the sun.

149. PLANES, TRAINS, OR AUTOMOBILES?

When traveling, if your destination is less than 300 miles away, it's best to avoid short-haul flights and opt for a different mode of transportation. According to the World Wildlife Fund, short-haul flights are the least fuel-efficient way of travel. Choosing to drive or going by bus or train are the most eco-friendly ways when you don't have too far to go. And when you do have to travel far, choose planes with the highest possible occupancy rates: it means they are the most fuel-efficient for the fleet of planes.

150. COFFEE FOR THE ROAD

Don't reach for air fresheners to deodorize your ride. All chemical air fresheners do is mask the odor, not neutralize whatever is making the unpleasant scent. One trick dealers of used cars use is freshly ground coffee beans. Just leave a bowl of coffee grounds in the car and let the odors absorb into the grounds. The coffee acts like a filter, cleaning the air and absorbing the smelly particles right into the coffee grounds. The longer you let them sit, the better they will work.

151. READ (AND RECYCLE) ALL ABOUT IT!

Glossy paper can be hard to recycle, but not all shiny paper is necessarily a nonrecyclable. Magazines and catalogs are recyclable because the paper stock is coated with a white clay that makes the pages appear more brilliant. That shiny surface from the clay does not interfere with the recycling process. According to Waste Management, about 45 percent of all magazines/catalogs are recycled today, which means more than half are still being tossed into the trash. Recycle away!

152. PICK THE PERFECT PETALS

Did you know many exotic flowers sold at the supermarket or by florists come from faraway places like China and South America? Florals are often flown in on gas-guzzling planes due to the flowers' short life span. So if you think flowers that have more frequent flier miles than you do are crazy, think about buying local flowers instead. To find locally grown flowers, use the website Local Harvest (localharvest.org) to find nearby growers. Just type in your zip code and a list of local farmers, farms, and retail stores will pop up.

153. A STARCHY SITUATION

Anything we can do to extend the life of our clothes is better for the environment. One way to start is to avoid spray starch. Spray starch may help you achieve a crisp shirt when ironing, but it can also be a tasty treat for insects like silverfish. The reality is that spray starch is just that: a food source. And when you use spray starch on fabrics, it attracts bugs. Over time, these insects will nibble away at your clothes and leave tears, holes, and damage. If you must use starch, keep your clothing in airtight containers. Or just give it up altogether: modern-day irons can freshen, remove wrinkles, and give crisp lines, using just water and heat.

154. KEEP IT SIMPLE

While buying an undyed, unbleached organic cotton T-shirt is the absolute greenest kind of T-shirt purchase, it isn't always the easiest to find. Instead, do the next best thing: choose white T-shirts over colored shirts. A typical T-shirt requires about 6.6 gallons of water to dye and process from white to a colored shirt. Choosing a conventional white T-shirt helps save water, reduces chemical dyes, and saves energy. If everyone did this, we'd save billions of gallons of water, too.

155. SHAKE IT UP

It's important to clean the inside of your reusable water bottles to remove grime, mildew, and bacteria. But getting a brush through a narrow opening can be very difficult. Instead of buying a brush, fill the bottle with a mixture of white vinegar and water and fill halfway up. Then add several ice cubes and screw on the cap. Shake vigorously. The vinegar will disinfect and the ice will agitate inside, loosening any mess. Dump, rinse with water, and voila! A perfectly clean water bottle.

156. COLOR CHANGE

If you use an inkjet printer, you know that it can be expensive to replace cartridges when the ink starts to run low. Given that black is the most popular color used when printing, it's the first to start to fade or streak when you're printing out documents. If this is the case, change the color of the text on your document from black to dark blue. This will switch the cartridges to a different ink and extend the life of your cartridges; you'll get dozens more pages with this simple hack.

157. WATERFRONT WASHING

During the summer months, you may find yourself taking advantage of an outdoor shower that's close to a beach or garden. If you do shower outdoors, remember to use soap and bath products sparingly. Any soap and bath products you use should be biodegradable, so that the soap mixture will break down in the soil where the shower drains. Just keep in mind that just because a product is labeled biodegradable, it doesn't mean it's *good* for the planet. Good options to look for are products made from pure castile soap; just a few drops can clean you from head to toe.

158. IN THE MAIL

If you hate standing in lines, here's a fast and eco-friendly way to get your postal supplies sent right to your home. You can order things like postage stamps, envelopes, boxes, and other supplies from the United States Postal Service website. Given that the post office is working 6 days a week delivering mail, they're going to be in your neighborhood anyway, which means they can bring you all your postal supplies. So this is a fast and easy to get what you need and to have it delivered without extra fuel being wasted to bring it to you.

159. PEEL AWAY

If you've ever wondered whether those gift boxes with the thin plastic "window" front are recyclable or not, the good news is that, yes, they are. But you have to do just one thing to prepare them for recycling. The paperboard boxes are recyclable in most curbside programs. But leaving the plastic on can be a problem for recyclers because it can muck up the recyclables during the pulping process. Before you recycle the box, peel off the plastic sheet (it's usually barely adhered on) and toss that in the trash. Then flatten the box for recycling!

160. BOXING DAY

Moving? When you're in need of cardboard boxes, you can get sticker shock when it comes to buying them. And why use brand-new boxes when you can recycle old ones? You can score free moving boxes with a little research and ingenuity in your community. Websites like FreeCycle and Craigslist are always good places to check; use the "Wanted" section to ask for boxes. And U-Haul has a service called "Customer Connect" that lets you search for free moving boxes near you. All you do is enter your zip code to find those who have boxes to give.

161. TWIST OFF

Plastic lids on things like juice, soda, and water bottles are now recyclable, but they should not be screwed tightly on the bottle. The reason is that when plastic bottles are compressed during the baling process, a tightly screwed-on lid or cap can prevent bottles from compressing. The solution? Leave the cap on the bottle, but ever so barely on. That way, it won't go astray in the recycling process and it'll allow the bottle to compress at the recycling facility.

162. TRASH IT

When you have a container of lighter fluid or motor oil, you might notice that the plastic container it comes in is stamped with a #2 recycling symbol. And while that's a commonly recycled plastic, these containers are not. The reason is simple: plastic containers that have held flammable liquids are not recyclable. The residual oil inside can create something called a "flash point," and it also changes the overall chemical composition of the plastic. So, what to do? Safely dispose of these containers in the trash.

163. RECYCLE RIGHT

A tube of toothpaste is typically packaged in something called LDPE, or #4 plastic. This is becoming a more commonly accepted type of recyclable plastic, but curbside recyclers don't often list it as an example of an item they accept. If your recycler takes plastics marked #4, you can recycle your tube of toothpaste as long as it's clean. That's easy: all you have to do is snip the end with scissors and get the last bits of toothpaste out (use it to scrub your pearly whites clean!). Then toss it into the bin.

164. WET CLEAN

You see a dry cleaner with a sign outside that says they are "organic," so you assume: that's a green thing, right? Not so fast. In this case, it's not about organically grown plant products; the term is actually used to describe organic chemicals. Petroleum, for example, is considered "organic." If you want a truly eco-friendly "dry cleaning" method, look for those who do "wet" cleaning; it's gentle on most fabrics and it's free of harsh chemicals.

165. CORRECT YOUR LENS

It's believed that up to 20 percent of the 45 million people who wear disposable contact lenses flush them down the toilet. While it may not seem like a big deal to have the tiny plastic lenses go down the drain, it ends up leading to significant ocean pollution. The lenses break down and become "microplastics," which marine life mistake for food and eat. This ultimately not only poisons marine life, but it can end up in our food supply as well. If you wear contacts, dispose of them in the trash.

166. SAFETY FIRST

When you rinse out a steel or tin can for recycling, you might wonder: is the lid recyclable? The short answer is yes. It's made from the same material as the body of the can. But gently touch the sides of the lid and see if the edges are razor sharp or not. Even modern-day recycling facilities still do much sorting of recyclables by hand, and sharp edges may injure workers. To recycle a lid, shove it into the can and push against the edges of the top opening so it narrows. It prevents the lid from falling out and lets you recycle the entire can, lid and all.

A GREENER WORLD AROUND YOU

167. CATCH MY DRIFT

If you burn firewood, you know it's important not to incinerate things like pressure-treated wood, cardboard, and plywood, given that they can release a significant amount of toxins into the air when burned. But did you know that it's also imperative to avoid burning driftwood? Even though it came from a tree and simply tumbled in the ocean, driftwood also acts like a sponge. So when you burn it, all those absorbed chemicals it collected in ocean water get released when added to your beach fire pit.

168. SECOND TIME AROUND

Buying secondhand clothes at thrift stores or consignment shops isn't just easy on the wallet—it is also 95 percent more efficient than buying it new. The amount of energy used to make new clothes as opposed to reselling clothes is significantly less the second time around. A bonus tip: when you're shopping at a consignment store and you find the perfect-fitting jacket or pants, ask the store to hold items from that seller for you the next time they bring in clothes to sell. This seller is a perfect match to your body size, so future items should fit you perfectly, too.

169. REFUSE REFUSE

Reduce, reuse, recycle, and … refuse? Yes, refuse. We've been taught to be polite, and often we think it's rude to refuse the stack of napkins, plastic utensils, or plastic bags we're offered at takeout and stores. But if you don't want it, why take it? Learn to make a habit of ordering things and adding "I don't need a bag" or "No straw or napkins for me, please." The reality is, it's not considered rude to refuse things that will end up in the trash. And if it's a small business, they'll probably appreciate it more because they're saving money, too.

170. ON SECOND THOUGHT

Buying used is an eco-friendly choice, but it's not always the best one. When it comes to products designed to protect you, you should think twice about buying used. For babies and small children, never buy a used car seat. There is no way of knowing the history of the seat or if it's been recalled for safety issues. If you can't afford a new car seat, there are nonprofit programs that can help get one often for free. And secondly, never buy a used bike helmet. Once the helmet has been involved in a crash, it's compromised and won't protect your head as effectively as if it was new.

171. BOOK CLUB

If you plan on visiting a destination for a long period of time, consider becoming a temporary member of the public library in the city you're visiting. Instead of buying new books and bringing them with you, visit a local library at the start of your trip to borrow books! Then return them before you head home. It's free and it significantly lightens your load when you travel.

172. ROUND AND ROUND

It's so simple: Use rotating doors when visiting stores and office buildings. Rotating doors help prevent heat and air conditioning from escaping from the building. Using a regular door can create a vacuum effect, and cold air (in winter) or hot air (in summer) is then forced into the building, which means more energy is needed to heat or cool the inside air.

173. FUEL UP

Here's a quick tip to get the most out of filling up at the gas pump. If you see a tanker truck at your gas station filling up their reserves, just drive right on by. The reason is the tanker truck is filling up the reserves with a mixture of gasoline that can stir up other unknown sediment, dirt, or other debris that may be inside the tank. When the truck isn't there, those materials settle, but when the truck is filling up the tank, they rise to the top. That means it can end up in your own gas tank and cause problems for your car, like a clogged fuel filter.

174. GREATER GIFT

Did you know close to 40 percent of holiday gifts are returned to the stores by their recipients? But did you also know that 18 percent of gifts are donated to charity, another 15 percent are re-gifted, and a whopping 11 percent of gifts are simply tossed into the trash? That means only about 15 percent of gifts received each holiday season are actually kept and enjoyed. To help cut the waste, consider scrapping giving gifts that are too personal to give, like clothes, toys, and kitchen and bath items. Instead, think about experiential items like excursions to restaurants, a delicious bottle of organic wine, or even a donation in the recipient's name to a charity they support. We can cut the waste and give gifts that are a joy to give and a real joy to receive.

A GREENER WORLD AROUND YOU

175. GLASS ACT

Glass bottles, jars, and wineglasses may all be made from glass, but that doesn't mean that they are all recyclable. While glass jars and bottles that once held pantry staples like pasta sauce, ketchup, and applesauce are recyclable in your curbside recycling, other glass items used for bakeware and for table settings are not. The reason is this type of glass has a different melting point than other glass, which means tossing a chipped wineglass into your recycling bin can actually contaminate a load of recyclables. So, if you have glassware to get rid of, donate and don't recycle.

176. FREE UPGRADE

Did you know the average size of a recycling bin is 65 gallons? It's the standard size most trash haulers provide. If you're recycling more and making less trash, ask for an upgrade. Requesting a 95-gallon recycling bin is usually free, and all it takes is a simple phone call to get it from your recycling service. And while you're at it, if you downsize your garbage bin, many trash haulers will also reduce the price of your monthly service fee. Make less trash, save more cash!

177. CAP IT OFF

Did you know that metal bottle caps are recyclable but often tossed into the trash at recycling facilities? It's because they are too small and often end up as waste as the recyclables get sorted. So what to do? Start by opening a steel can (like a soup can) and an aluminum can (such as a soda). Start collecting any steel and aluminum bottle caps and sort them into the matching can. (If a cap sticks to a magnet, it's steel; if not, it's aluminum.) When the cans are full, just crimp them closed so nothing falls out, and then recycle in your curbside recycling bin.

178. BETTER BEACHES

Of the 6 million tons of trash that end up dumped in the world's oceans every year, about 80 percent of that is plastic. As a major threat to aquatic wildlife, plastic food packaging from six-pack rings, cling wrap, and plastic sandwich bags are often inadvertently dumped on beaches by beachgoers. Even if the trash is deposited into a receptacle, a strong gust of wind or an overflowing trash bin can still lead to litter on beaches and in the water. Bring this trash home to properly dispose of or—even better—use reusable items for everything.

179. BULK BUYING

Did you know that with the growth of online shopping, the amount of cardboard generated for just a year of deliveries in New York City can fill the Empire State Building 50,000 times? The simplest way to help cut back on packaging waste is to avoid buying *one* thing online that then requires a box, packaging material, and fuel to get it to you. Instead, fill your virtual shopping cart over time and try to get multiple items together in one box. Or better yet, buy it from a local business and try to buy online only when you absolutely must.

180. PARTY TIME

Are you planning to throw an event for lots of guests? Instead of buying all new tableware, flatware, glasses, napkins, and other linens, why not rent them instead? If you're renting a venue for the event, check with them and they might have rental companies they typically work with. The party renting process has been made easy with websites that literally put everything you need to throw a party in a box. And when you're done, you just pack it all back up and send it to them. By renting, you save resources by reusing items, and you also save money because you don't have to buy everything new.

181. GO DIRECT

While flying around the country on a plane is not an environmentally friendly thing to do, sometimes you just can't prevent it. But there are things you can do to lighten your carbon footprint when you do fly. First, look for nonstop flights or direct routes to where you're going. A whopping 25 percent of a plane's fuel usage is used during takeoff, so the more you take off and land, the more fuel is wasted. You can also choose fuel-efficient aircrafts; it turns out that Airbus A350-900 and Boeing 787-9 are the greenest planes around.

182. BROWSE BETTER

Whenever you make a Teams call, do an internet search, or buy something online, you use energy beyond just what your phone or laptop is drawing. These bytes of information come from a data center where tons of energy is consumed to keep this constant demand for information available. In fact, these centers currently use a whopping 2 percent of the world's energy. Some easy ways to help: stop cc'ing everyone on emails and try compressing attachments to lessen the strain. Use ad blockers when searching online, which can reduce energy strain, too.

183. FASHION WEAK

According to Greenpeace, we are wearing clothing about five times less often before it's thrown away or donated than we've done in the past. It's because of something called "fast fashion," which is inexpensive and cheaply made clothing that simply doesn't last very long. Turns out, cheaply made duds now equal about 80 billion pieces of clothing made every single year. A simple question to ask yourself when shopping for clothes: will you wear it at least 30 times? If not, it's best to pass and move on. Or buy lightly used clothes from resell sites or stores, for the absolute greenest choice.

184. REDUCE, REUSE, REPLAY

Do you use Apple AirPods? Turns out the wireless buds use a small rechargeable battery to function. Over time, that battery can die, and it's nearly impossible to replace it. Instead of recycling your dead AirPods at Apple and buying a pricey new pair, you can save money by simply using a service that refurbishes them for you. PodSwap takes your old pair and sends you a refurbished brand-new set at a fraction of the cost. They'll fix your old ones and find a new home for those when they're done repairing them.

185. REROUTING

If you're planning to travel to see family during the holiday season, be sure to pick a time to drive that will have less congestion, to help cut back on fuel waste (and personal aggravation). Turns out driving in stop-and-go traffic on the highway can significantly lower your fuel efficiency by as much as 30 percent. Also, try using real-time GPS devices on your phone (which uses real traffic conditions to route you efficiently to your destination), which can also save you another 10 percent in gas mileage because it gives you the best possible scenario to get from point A to point B.

186. PLAY TIME

If you own sneakers that are past the point of repair or donation, you don't have to throw them in the trash. Nike has been recycling athletic shoes since 1993 as part of a program called Reuse-a-Shoe that grinds up old sneakers into a material called "Nike Grind." It's used to make soft surfaces in playgrounds, soccer fields, and basketball courts. They take *any* brand of sneaker, and they can be dropped off at any Nike store in the United States for free. Since 1992, over 140 million pounds of "Nike Grind" have been recycled into new products.

187. SAFER SORTING

Despite advances in recycling that use machines to sort out recyclables, a good majority of the process is still done manually by people. That's why it's so important to be diligent about what you place in your recycling bin. Items like medical waste, old medication, needles, and animal waste should never be placed in the bin because it puts workers at risk.

188. GREENER RIDE

If you use a rideshare program like Uber to get around town, did you know you can make your ride greener? Uber Green is a new option that lets you opt for drivers of hybrid and electric vehicles. These low-emission rides can get you around town nicely, and the rate is usually the same as the least expensive Uber X prices. All you have to do is opt for this type of car when you're on the app to take advantage of it.

189. BAD CREDIT (CARD COMPANY)

Do you know who one of the biggest sellers of names and addresses, resulting in your mailbox being flooded with junk mail, is? It's your credit card company. If you're tired of the 5 million tons of junk mail that are sent to Americans every year (and end up in landfills), you can help significantly decrease that amount by simply contacting your credit card companies. Ask them to opt you out of any third-party mailing lists. And while you're at it, sign up at OptOutPreScreen.com to remove your name for five years from the list for receiving new credit card offers in the mail, too.

190. FILL 'ER UP

We're all trying to save money at the gas pump, and there are some small things you can do to maximize your savings and your car's fuel efficiency. One of the easiest things is to wait until your car's gas tank is at least one-quarter full (or less) before filling up again. The reason is that when your car is carrying less fuel around, it's lighter and therefore more fuel-efficient. And adding gas just a few dollars at a time is also inefficient; the fewer trips you need to make to the gas station, the less fuel is wasted.

191. SAND FREE

Even accidentally taking a little bit of sand from the beach (stray sand that ends up in sneakers or at the bottoms of bags) can add up to significant erosion when you multiply that by the number of people who visit every single day. To help prevent accidental sand loss, try these tips. Start with a mesh tote bag, so sand can easily fall through the hole. Avoid sneakers and closed-toe shoes; choose flip-flops, which can be easily shaken clean. And choose a chair over a beach towel for lounging; chairs can easily be dipped into the water, so any sand can be washed off.

192. CHEERS TO THAT

If you drink carbonated beverages, which is better? A plastic bottle or aluminum cans? The answer is simple: aluminum. According to the EPA, aluminum cans are one of the most commonly recycled materials. In less than 60 days, a typical soda can goes from the supermarket to the recycling bin to the recycling facility and is back on the shelf as a new soda can. This recycling process can be done indefinitely because aluminum is durable, unlike plastic, which can only be recycled a few times before being discarded into a landfill.

193. KEEP IT LOOSE

It's almost universal that every recycling program in the United States has this rule: do not bag your recyclables. Plastic bags are the #1 contaminant in recycling collections and should be avoided at all costs. In fact, some recycling facilities have rules that if a bag comes to the facility full of recyclables, it is deemed "trash" and workers are barred from opening the bag, even if it is clearly full of recyclables. Instead, let your recyclables stay commingled and unbagged when you recycle.

194. BEAUTY SECRET

Another reason to ditch disposable plastic water bottles: they can make you look older. New reports show the pursing of the lips around a bottle of water repeatedly can actually form deep wrinkles around our lips. The look is similar to a lifelong smoker who also purses their lips around a cigarette. To avoid having older looking lips, keep drinking water but do it from a glass. Just another reason to invest in an inexpensive water filtration system at home and to skip the ecological nightmare of plastic bottled water.

195. PIT STOP

We've all done this: you drop someone off in front of a store so they can run and grab something quickly, while you sit there and let the car idle. If the errand is less than 10 seconds, that's fine, but any more and you're wasting gas. That's a fact according to the Environmental Defense Fund, who says motorists who sit idle for more than 10 seconds are wasting more fuel and money than if they just turned it off and restarted the engine.

196. HYPER ON HYPO

Don't confuse the word "hypoallergenic" to mean eco-friendly when buying products like skin care and bedding. The reality is the word *hypoallergenic* only means it won't trigger allergic reactions. It's not a classification that means the product is natural, eco-friendly, or organic at all. But even worse: there is no regulation from the US government what the word *hypoallergenic* actually means, so anyone can really slap the word on any product. Read labels and learn if the actual ingredients and materials used live up to your green expectations.

197. HOTEL, MOTEL

According to the Environmental Protection Agency, of the 47,000 hotels and motels in the United States, about $2,196 is spent per room each year on energy costs. That equals about 6 percent of all hotel operating costs for a hotel. When staying at a hotel, follow the same mindful habits you do at home: when you leave a room or check out, turn off the thermostat or significantly lower or raise it based on the time of year to save energy. If you notice a leak in the bathroom, report it to the front desk. The more we all do to lower energy usage, the lower hotel rates will become and it becomes win-win for everyone all around.

198. KEEP IT COOL

Old sponges and freezer bags can be given a second life as freezer packs. First, disinfect your old sponge in the microwave by heating it on high (while wet) for 90 seconds. When it is cool, soak it in water and place it inside a freezer bag. Freeze for a few hours until it is frozen solid. Place it in shopping bags when you grocery shop and it will help keep frozen food cold longer. As the ice melts, the sponge will automatically reabsorb the water, too.

199. WIPER WASTE

Do the math: with nearly 250 million cars on the road in the United States, all those sprays of windshield washer fluid add up. It turns out the majority of them are made of methanol, which is so toxic that just two tablespoons can kill a child if ingested. With so many cars spraying to clean their windshields, the accumulation of droplets on roads ends up in waterways and in our environment. Instead, take the time to buy biodegradable fluid that's methanol-free the next time you refill your car.

200. KEEP IT SQUEAKY

Car washes do more than keep your car looking clean, they also help protect it in the long run. All the dirt, grime, and other debris that end up on the exterior of your car can slowly create microscopic scratches that eat away at your vehicle's paint. The more tears, the more chances the raw metal underneath will become exposed and form rust on the metal. Regular car washing can help keep your car in tip-top shape so you'll be less likely to upgrade your vehicle in coming years.

201. DON'T MIX IT UP

Paper is paper, right? When recycling old office paper, magazines, and other recyclable paper, you'd be surprised to learn that shredded paper is not a desired recyclable, even if it is recyclable in a pre-shredded form. Because a recycler can't always tell what was shredded when they receive bales of shredded paper, it can make it hard to recycle. Sometimes glossy, shiny paper gets mixed in along with plastic report covers and metal pieces, which contaminates the load of recyclables. When it's all shredded, you can't tell what's what. Instead, tear recyclable paper and save the shredding for truly confidential docs that you dispose of in the trash.

202. BUGGED OUT

We drag our suitcases, carry-on bags, and back packs all over the country (or world) when we travel, and when we get home, we wash all our clothes but don't think twice about the actual bag it was carried in. The reality is: one of the easiest ways to give bed bugs a free ride into your home is through your luggage. To see if your bags have bed bugs, blow a hair dryer all over them. Use slow and steady motions to blow hot air along the edges and corners of the bag. Because bed bugs do not like heat, they will start to show themselves. If you see any bugs, take steps to fully disinfect your bag outside the home before bringing it back indoors.

203. PHOTO FINISH

Can you recycle old printed photographs with your scrap paper recycling? Yes and no. It all depends on how the photo was printed. If it was done in an old-fashioned chemical processing fashion, then no. If it was printed using modern digital technology, then yes. How do you find out? Simply tear it; if the photograph rips with a very clean tear, it can be recycled. If it's hard to tear and rips in layers and not so cleanly, you likely have a nonrecyclable photo that needs to be thrown in the trash and not the recycling bin.

204. REUSE AND REUSE

An interesting study by the Institute of Lifecycle Analysis figured out how many times you needed to reuse a reusable cup before it actually begins to save energy and resources in comparison to using a throwaway paper cup over time. When compared to a typical paper coffee cup, they found a reusable ceramic mug would need to be used 39 times before you begin to see environmental savings, a plastic thermos would need to be used 17 times, and a heat-resistant glass mug just 15 times. What's taken in to consideration is the amount of materials and resources needed to make a reusable cup plus the amount of water and energy to wash it. So don't get caught up in the cup craze. Only buy one reusable cup and use it over and over and over.

205. SUPER SELLER

The resale market for clothing is hotter than ever, with sites like eBay, TheRealReal, and Poshmark helping consumers find new homes (and cash) for their lightly worn clothes. When reselling clothing, there are a few things you can do to maximize your profits. First, take plenty of photos showing the front, back, and even any tears, stains, or marks to help manage buyers' expectations. Then download a measurement chart from the clothing brand's website and post it in your listing; because sizes differ from brand to brand, this will help customers fully understand the fit of the item.

206. FORE!

If you play golf, you may want to consider the type of golf ball you use if you're playing near water. Even though traditional golf balls will sink to the bottom of the pond, over time they will begin to degrade and microparticles of plastic will end up in the water. New innovations have been made in golf balls that are designed to biodegrade safely in water and even leave behind fish food for aquatic wildlife. Of course, the best bet: improve your game and avoid waterways altogether!

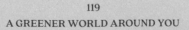

207. DON'T MAKE A WISH

Have you heard of "wish-cycling"? It's when someone is so passionate about recycling they toss items into the recycling bin "wishing" it was recyclable and hoping someone else can figure out at the recycling facility if it can be recycled. While it's nice to have an optimistic viewpoint on recycling, this is actually more like down-cycling. When questionable recyclables get tossed into the bin, it costs time and money for these items to be sorted out and tossed away. When in doubt, toss it out.

CHAPTER 3

FOOD FOR THOUGHT

We all know the old saying: You are what you eat. True enough. But consider this twist: What you eat—not to mention where and how you eat it—impacts the broader world as well. Making informed decisions about food choices can mean better health for you and the planet. Talk about a win-win!

This roundup of tips covers sourcing, cooking, and storing food. By making a few smart changes, you'll eat healthier and stretch your grocery budget. It's all food for thought, but each one of these tips is also easy to do.

208. ROAD TRIP

Hitting the road for a trip can sometimes feel like your food options are limited to fast food joints at rest stops along the way. But it's possible to find local, sustainable, and even organic food on your journey. The Eat Well Guide is an online tool that uses your two destination points—from where you start to where you end—and gives you healthy, sustainable options for where to dine on your trip. Or, if you're visiting a city and want greener cuisine options, you can just list a single address to find the closest listings. Visit EatWellGuide.org to start your culinary journey today.

209. CHEERS!

When wine comes from faraway places like France, South America, and Australia, it means it takes a lot of fuel to ship those heavy pallets of vino to your local wine store. Wine shouldn't have more frequent flier miles than you do, so think locally made wines the next time you sip. The free app Winery Passport has over 4,500 wineries you can search through. Just type in your geographic details (like zip code) and they'll pinpoint local winemakers closest to you. It also includes the addresses, types of vintages they sell and make, and even reviews on the wines from other connoisseurs.

210. COOK LIKE A STAR

If you're in the market for a new set of pots and pans, consider copper-bottomed pots and pans. Turns out copper metal is the best conductor of heat and creates an even and more efficient cooking surface. The more even the heat, the faster the cooking time, the less energy you use to whip up dinner. Also, test the lids on your new pots to make sure they are tight-fitting. A loose lid will waste energy and take more time when doing things like bringing water to a boil.

211. TAKE OUT

Can you recycle a greasy pizza box with your cardboard recyclables? Yes and no. If a portion of the box is covered in grease, cheese, and other food debris, it can contaminate a load of recyclable cardboard if you try to recycle it. Instead, tear off the greasy part and only recycle the clean cardboard. But here's a tip to prevent greasy boxes: Ask the pizzeria to place a sheet of aluminum foil on the bottom of the box, then put the pizza on top. This helps keep the grease from seeping into the cardboard plus it keeps the pizza hotter for longer. And don't forget: if the aluminum foil is clean enough, just crumple it up and toss it into the recycling bin. It's recyclable!

212. SAFE CITRUS

It's okay to buy conventionally grown lemons if you can't find organic. It just depends on what you plan to do with them. If you're just using the juice of the lemon, it's okay to go with conventionally grown. But if you plan on using the zest of a lemon—the skin or peel—always go with organically grown citrus, given that you're eating the outside of the lemon. Organic lemons are grown without pesticides, so the zest is safe to use for cooking. But even with organic, be sure you wash it well: lemons—conventional and organic—have been touched by many hands before they reach your supermarket. It's just good food safety to wash them before use.

213. BULKING UP

Buying in bulk from wholesale clubs can be a great way to save money and reduce packaging on some of your favorite everyday items. But be careful to avoid buying perishable foods in bulk like ketchup, mustard, mayo, and other condiments. The reason is most families will not go through the entire supply before it goes bad; dollar for dollar, it's better to buy these items in normal-size jars. One other item to avoid? Brown rice. Brown rice only has a shelf life of 6 months because it retains its natural oils and fatty acids; when it goes bad, it takes on a rancid taste. White rice, which is free of those fats, has a shelf life of 30 years.

214. CHEERS!

When it comes to beer, is it better to go with aluminum or glass-packaged brews? The answer? Aluminum. While both materials are easily recyclable, turns out the likelihood that an aluminum can put into the recycling stream will actually get recycled is much higher than glass. And while it does take more energy to mine and make cans, they are infinitely recyclable, lighter to transport, and worth more to recyclers. Of course, skipping a single-use cup and drinking from the can or bottle is best, too.

215. BLACK, WHITE, AND RED (APPLES) ALL OVER

When left on a kitchen counter, fresh apples can last for as little as 2 days before going bad. Try this genius trick instead: wrap each apple in a small piece of newspaper. Wrapping the apple in newspaper helps prevent apples from bruising each other; when they do bruise, it speeds up the ripening process and turns fresh apples into rotten ones very quickly. After wrapping each apple, place them in a cardboard box and store them in a cool dark place like a refrigerator or a basement and they'll stay fresh for several weeks.

DO JUST ONE THING

216. PUT A (REAL) CORK IN IT

We all know easy plastics to avoid like plastic straws, single-use bags, and disposable cups, but did you know there some less obvious things to be aware about? When it comes to wine, not all stoppers are the same. Some use natural cork stoppers (which are biodegradable) and others use plastic. To know if your favorite bottle uses a real cork or not, a website called CorkWatch (recork.com/corkwatch) can help you find out. According to CorkWatch, "buying bottles with natural cork promotes cork harvesting, which extends the lifespan of cork trees and supports the conservation of over 6.7 million acres of ecologically sensitive cork forests."

217. GIVE 'EM A RINSE

It isn't always possible to only buy and eat organic fruits and vegetables, so when you do buy conventional produce, give it a good soak to remove all the residual pesticides. Fill your clean kitchen sink with cold water and add about 1 cup of white vinegar. Soak your produce—things like grapes, berries, and broccoli—for 10 minutes. The natural acid in the white vinegar helps break down the chemical coatings. You will be shocked at how foggy the water will become.

218. NOT DOWN THE DRAIN

You might think tossing leftover food into the garbage disposal is better than throwing it into the trash (which goes to the landfill). But you're wrong: all those fruit peels, eggshells, and veggie trims still end up in the trash, even if they go down the drain. Water-treatment facilities skim waste out of our water supply and dispose of it in landfills. So, using a garbage disposal is no better than throwing it out. Instead, invest in a sinkside composting container and empty organic matter into a backyard compost bin whenever possible.

219. AL DENTE!

Every little bit counts when it comes to saving energy! Here's a simple Do Just One Thing: turn off the stove a few minutes before your food is done cooking. When making pasta, bring a pot of water to a boil and then add pasta. Turn off the heat and put a lid on top of the pot. Add about 5 more minutes to the pasta cook time and you'll get perfectly cooked al dente pasta every single time and will save energy and money. And remember: cooled pasta water is nutrient-rich water your outdoor plants will love.

220. AN OILY SITUATION

One of the worst enemies of good oils like olive, grapeseed, and avocado oil is ultraviolet light. When the sun's rays hit your kitchen counter full of clear oils, it begins to deteriorate the contents of the bottles. When shopping for oils, look for opaque containers instead. The dark containers block the UV light and help keep your oils fresher for longer. And don't store them near your kitchen stove: the heat from cooking can also break down oils.

221. FRESH FLOURS

If you're a baker, there's nothing worse than going to your pantry and finding flour that's gone rancid. When you open bags of flour at home, transfer the contents out of the bag and into an airtight container. And store the flour in the freezer. According to the Wheat Foods Council, flour can last indefinitely if frozen. In the fridge, it can stay fresh for a whole two years.

222. THE MILKY WAY

If you have some milk in the fridge that's spoiled or whose freshness is questionable, don't pour it down the drain. The great thing about milk is that it's loaded with nutrition including calcium, protein, vitamin B, and natural sugars that are also good for plants. Use old milk as an all-natural fertilizer by pouring it around the base of plants in the garden to give them a nutritional boost. The micro-organisms in the soil will love it, too, which in the long term helps to improve the overall health of the soil.

223. PORTION CONTROLS

According to the Natural Resources Defense Council, an astounding 40 percent of food in the United States ends up in the landfill. To help cut back on food waste, try this simple tip to save leftovers at home. Invest in reusable, small flat containers with matching lids and divide leftovers into smaller containers. This will help the food cool down faster and prevent bacteria spores from germinating more than if it were stored in one large container. The benefit of several containers also helps with portion control, so family members can opt to reheat one container as opposed to an entire batch of food.

224. ICE IS NOT NICE

The refrigerator is one of the biggest energy hogs in the house, so it's key to make sure it runs efficiently to save electricity and money. If you don't use your automatic ice maker often, consider turning it off. A study by *Time* magazine found that the average ice maker increases energy usage by 12 to 20 percent. By simply turning it off, you'll significantly improve efficiency. Want ice? Consider filling silicone ice cube trays with water and using them instead of an automatic ice maker.

225. A COVER UP

When storing leftovers in the refrigerator, it's imperative to cover the food to keep it fresh. But did you know covering your food also helps you save energy? A refrigerator has something called a compressor, and its job is to keep the air inside the fridge cool. Moist air in the refrigerator is harder to keep cool, so the compressor has to work harder. Uncovered food emits moisture, and over time, it uses more energy. Investing in reusable silicone covers or foil to cover food is a simple and easy way to help.

226. HOLY GRAIN

If you're making yourself a sandwich today, consider whole grain breads over white bread for your BLT. To turn flour into "white" flour for bread, it goes through a whole series of refining processes that use a significant amount of energy to get the job done. By choosing a whole grain or wheat bread, you're selecting a less-processed ingredient that therefore is more sustainable (and in this columnist's humble opinion, more flavorful).

227. CRAVING RAISINS?

Here's a reason to always buy organic raisins: conventional brands often fumigate raisins with toxic gases to prevent pests from destroying them in storage. According to the Environmental Working Group, it's not just the chemicals used on grapes in the field that are concerning but also the fumigant residue, which could pose health risks to you and your family (not to mention farm workers and people in the manufacturing facility). And with 208 million pounds of raisins eaten by kids every year, choosing organic is a healthier and proactive step to make sure these chemicals don't end up in their cereal bowl or favorite cookie, too.

228. FOREVER FOODS

It's staggering: nearly half of the food grown or produced in the world is wasted. And often it's from food that expired and is no longer safe for consumption. But you can prioritize purchasing foods that actually never expire or have a longer shelf life. Honey, for example, never expires: there is a natural chemistry from the bees that turns nectar into one of the most perfect foods that can last forever. And condiments like salt, soy sauce, and real maple syrup can be added to the list of forever-foods. Maple syrup is naturally antimicrobial and will stay sweet for as long as you have it.

229. KEEP IT SEPARATE

Do you use a number of condiments like mayonnaise, mustard, and other spreads when making a sandwich or homemade salad dressing? One of the easiest ways to contaminate all those jars and bottles is by using the same utensil each time you scoop out a spoonful. Because the shelf life for many condiments can be very long (about 3 years for mustard), the fastest way to spoil condiments is through cross contamination. Instead, make a habit to use separate spoons or at least to rinse it before dipping into another jar.

230. CHEERS TO SOFT SKIN

Ever open a bottle of red wine and a few days later, it's turned? There is no need to toss the leftover vino down the drain. Instead, pour it right into your bubble bath instead. Red wine has a natural ingredient called "antioxidant polyphenols" that have anti-aging properties. When you soak in a warm bubble bath with red wine, it helps soften and rejuvenate your skin (and it won't turn your skin red, either). Spoiled red wine can now equal soft, dewy skin.

231. PERSONAL PAN

Got leftover pizza? When you put a slice of 'za on a plate in the microwave, it never comes out the same way it did when it was fresh at the pizzeria. A trick to reheat that slice and have it remain hot, crispy, and almost fresh-tasting out of the oven is to cook it on a cooktop. Simply heat up a heavy pan (like a cast-iron pan) and place the slice of pizza in the pan. Let it warm up: it'll toast the crust, heat it up, and melt the cheese. In a few minutes, you've got a perfect crispy slice.

232. SUSTAINABLE SIPPING

The greenest way to enjoy a soda pop? Use a reusable cup and a soda fountain. While plastic, glass, and aluminum containers are all recyclable, they come with a similar number of cons to pros. Oil is used to make plastic bottles, and the resins are not infinitely recyclable. While glass is infinitely recyclable, it's heavier, so the carbon footprint to ship glass bottles is higher than plastic; plus, only 25 percent of glass bottles are actually recycled. And aluminum? While 50 percent of the can is recycled, the other 50 percent is virgin aluminum that comes from destructive mining practices. A reusable container that you bring and use over and over is the clear winner.

233. EASY FREEZE

When packing a lunch to take to the office or for your kid to take to school, try this hack to keep your food chilled. Freezing a container of yogurt does two things: it transforms it into an ice pack and keeps your yogurt cold until it's lunchtime. It's also the right type of ingredient to freeze. Freezing a juice container or thermos of water may work, but it's slow to thaw out. Dairy items (like yogurt) freeze hard, but thaw quickly. So by lunch, it'll be at the perfect creamy consistency you love.

234. SPA DAY

Instead of tossing your parsley stems into the compost bin, harness their natural deodorizing properties to create a soothing spa treatment instead. Parsley is loaded with chlorophyll, which is a powerful natural deodorizer and has antibacterial properties. While it's known as a natural breath freshener, it can also be an amazing astringent for your feet. Just fill a shallow bowl with hot water and add the parsley stems to the water. Let it steep and soak your feet for about 15 minutes. They'll come out refreshed, relaxed, and clean.

235. SUNNY DELIGHT

Plastic food storage containers provide a good reusable solution to keep leftovers fresh, but they can often stain. Even with hand-scrubbing in the sink or using a dishwasher, they can still stay stained or retain an odor that seems impossible to remove. On a very hot, sun-intensive day, try using the sun's rays to deodorize and brighten them instead. Wash them clean and place them on top of a towel in the yard (where it's the brightest). The UV rays from the sun will do their cleaning magic.

236. TEA TIME

If you love tea and wonder what to do with used tea bags, here are a few upcycling ideas: use it as a compress on a bruise, beesting, or sunburn to help provide relief and reduce inflammation. Or place a few used tea bags in a dirty casserole dish and add hot water. The residual tannins in the used tea bags will break down the grease to make cleaning up a breeze. Finally, when repotting plants, place a used tea bag at the drainage hole inside the pot. It will help retain water inside, release nutrients into the soil, and degrade into beneficial mulch over time.

237. H_2-NO

Here's another reason to quit drinking bottled water: it's often laced with plastic particles. Scientists recently tested a variety of national brand bottled waters and found 93 percent of them were contaminated with plastic. The plastic didn't come from polluted water sources but from the actual packaging to make the bottled water. When manufacturers cut plastic bottles and add caps, small fragments of plastic get cut and inadvertently added to the water. And this is how you end up accidentally ingesting plastic.

238. PICKY EATERS

Are your kids' lunches coming home half-eaten every day? They may not be avoiding certain foods, but simply have too much to eat. The reality is, there are appropriate food portions for kids of different ages. To find the right portion size, click on the website  choosemyplate.gov. It helps provide information on correct portion sizes for kids of every age. This will help you lessen food waste and save you money in the long run.

239. FAST (WASTE-FREE) FOOD

Did you know it's possible to eat at a fast-food restaurant without generating any waste? Subway is the one fast-food chain that actually wraps their sandwiches in paper that is fully compostable. If you look closely at the paper, it actually has the words "Please Compost" on the side. The trick is to order a sandwich and to ask for no plastic bag, no napkins, and—while you're at it— no receipt. Then you can enjoy your sandwich and compost the paper to create a zero-waste fast-food experience when you're on the go.

240. GUACA-HOLY-MOLY

When you slice open an avocado, don't toss the avocado skin into the trash or compost bin right away. The skin, which still has some avocado fruit and natural oils on the reverse side, is a fantastic instant beauty treatment for your skin. Simply massage the remnant avocado fruit and oils onto your face. It's rich in vitamin E and potassium, which helps feed dry skin. And the natural antioxidants in avocados help with dry and flaky skin and can help calm inflammation and acne-prone skin, too.

241. KEEP IT FRESH

Usually, a refrigerator is the ideal place to keep perishables fresh. But that's not the case for every fruit and vegetable. Never put potatoes in a refrigerator; the cool temperatures can easily turn the starch-rich vegetables into sugar bombs in no time flat. The same goes for tomatoes, which can go from sun-ripened goodness into flavorless mush. And fresh garlic and onions are also no-no's for your fridge; the cool temps turn them moldy and soft, and they are better off in a cool, dark place like your pantry or basement instead.

242. BEST BEETS

Did you buy a bunch of fresh beets and forget about them? There's no need to toss soft beets when they can easily be made crispy and crunchy again all with just a cup of water. Because beets are a root vegetable, they easily drink up water like sponges. Just fill a glass with cold water and let the beets soak in it for a day or two. These thirsty beets will drink it up, plump up, and be as good as new to use.

243. GREENER JUICE

Are you looking for a new juicer to make freshly squeezed juices at home? Consider a "gear" juicer instead of the "centrifugal" style. Here's why: A centrifugal juicer breaks up the molecules of the fruits and veggies, which means any chemical and bacterial residue ends up in the finished juice. A gear juicer presses produce without disrupting the molecules, which means more chemicals end up in the pulp and not the juice. But whichever model you choose, be sure always to wash your produce before use. Even organic produce has residual dirt and bacteria on it that can make you sick.

244. SUPERMARKET SWEEP

Do you know what hour of the day and day of the week is the cheapest time to stock up on organic fruits and vegetables at the supermarket? It's Wednesday night! On Tuesdays, supermarket circulars' advertising sales come out for sales starting on Wednesday. At night, supermarket managers take inventory of perishables and mark down items that are overstocked. Combine the weekly sale with the markdowns and you have a chance to score organic bargains every Wednesday night.

245. SQUEEZE THIS

Do you need just a little bit of freshly squeezed lemon juice? Don't waste an entire lemon; instead use this simple toothpick hack. Roll the lemon with the palm of your hand on the countertop. Then prick the lemon once with the toothpick. Now squeeze away. The small hole will allow fresh juice to be drained, all without having to cut the lemon open. The lemon will stay fresh longer, so it can still be used the next day.

246. HOMEMADE MASK

Is there some residual yogurt inside that plastic container? Don't rinse it out; use it to create a highly effective face mask. Turns out yogurt made from dairy milk has an active ingredient called lactic acid, which can help improve your skin's clarity. Just spoon out the leftover yogurt and smear it on your face, throat, and chest for about 15 minutes (a great thing to use before you shower). Then rinse it off. It's gentle enough to use daily, and you'll see results after just a few uses of this one-ingredient yogurt mask.

247. LAWN PARTY

Have a bunch of leftover beer from a party? Collect all the undrunk, flat beer and use it to give your dying lawn a nutritional boost. The facts are simple: beer is a fermented product that is loaded with natural sugars that your lawn loves. When you pour beer on dying or brown patches of grass, it acts like a fertilizer and gives weak spots a better chance to rejuvenate and absorb the nutrients they need to repair themselves. You can also speed up the decomposition process of your compost pile by pouring beer on top; the natural yeast and sugar will feed beneficial bacteria that creates compost.

248. SWEET SCENT

Have you ever wondered what you can do with an apple core? Turns out you can help deodorize a room. One simple thing is to simmer apple cores in water and let the natural scent permeate the air and leave behind a pleasant scent (you can also add a cinnamon stick to make it a more autumnal scent). But you can also just leave an apple core out where there's a lingering smell to help deodorize. As the core oxidizes, it rapidly absorbs the odors around it, so you'll be left with a fresh-smelling space!

249. A SLOW BURN

If you love pistachios, you're often left with a pile of shells when you snack on them. Don't throw the shells away. Old shells are slow burners because of the residual oil from the pistachio meat and are a perfect fire starter for the backyard grill or fire pit. Just scatter them at the base of whatever you're trying to ignite and light away.

250. PANTRY PRIORITIES

Even small amounts of excess moisture in the air can cause food spoilage, so it's imperative to make sure your pantry is as dry as possible. To see if your pantry passes the test, just tape a sheet of aluminum foil onto the wall where it faces an exterior side of the house (in other words, not a wall facing another room inside your home on its opposite side). Let that aluminum sheet stay put for a few days. Peel away the aluminum foil sheet and quickly examine it; if there is any condensation on the side that faced the wall, there is excess moisture lingering in your pantry. On the other side, it's excess moisture in the air.

251. GET SHREDDED

Not only is preshredded cheese from the supermarket expensive, but it also comes packaged in hard-to-recycle plastic packaging. One way to go green and save money is to buy blocks of cheese from the deli counter and shred it yourself. To save time, shred the entire block of cheese at the same time and store it in a large reusable silicone freezer bag. To prevent the shredded cheese from sticking together, add a tablespoon of cornstarch to the freezer bag and shake. It will lightly coat the cheese and prevent sticking and will also help keep the shredded cheese fresher longer.

252. TOP CHEF

How many times have you forgotten about something in your refrigerator only to realize it's spoiled or gone bad and you have to toss it out? Before running to the grocery store, try to get creative and use what's left in your fridge for a meal. Make it a challenge: do the "clear the shelf" game where you have to completely empty out a shelf to make a meal. It's easy to come up with crowd-pleasing meals like a soup, stir fries, or a frittata. You'll save money and have help cut down on food waste.

253. ICEBERG (LETTUCE) AHEAD!

Did you know the back of your refrigerator is the coldest? And sometimes it's a significant difference in temperature from, say, the front or compartments in the door itself. This is important to know when storing your most delicate produce, like lettuces, fresh herbs, and other greens like spinach and arugula. If you place these items near the back, they have a high likelihood of freezing, which can change their taste and texture. Keep these delicate greens up front so they're crisp, not frozen.

254. BACK IT UP

Do you keep that carton of milk or coffee creamer conveniently placed in your refrigerator door? Sure, it may be easier to grab and use it to add a splash to your coffee or cereal in the morning, but it's the last place you should be storing dairy. Real milk products need to be kept at a cold temperature, and the door is too warm to keep milk fresh. The best place? Store dairy in the back of the refrigerator, where the temperature is at its coldest.

255. IT'S ALL GOOD

When you have a whole head of cauliflower or broccoli, don't just eat the florets and dispose the stalk and leaves into the trash. The reality is the whole heads of both vegetables are totally edible. While a bit more tough, the stalks of both vegetables are nutritious and, if prepared properly, delicious! The stems can be chopped up finely to be added to a pesto or stew; thinly sliced and steamed or pan fried; and even grated to be used in salads or a coleslaw. And, of course, you can take the cut-up stalks and other vegetable trimmings to make homemade stock, too.

256. SAVE THE JUICE

Pickle brine juice is a fantastic ingredient you shouldn't toss down the drain after you've eaten the last dill. The easiest way to reuse it is to brine onions, garlic, or soft veggies (like cucumbers) to make instant pickles. You can also tenderize meat with it, boil potatoes in it (which adds a zingy flavor profile), and even give a homemade Bloody Mary some extra zing with a dash of pickle brine juice. Outside the kitchen, toss it onto stubborn weeds to naturally kill them.

257. FRESH BAKED

To keep bread fresh, the best and worst place to store it is in the refrigerator. For fresh bread you make yourself, the last place you should store the delicious sourdough is in the fridge; it can stale quickly in the cold, slightly moist environment. In fact, according to *Epicurious*, it can stale up to "six times faster than bread on the counter." But store-bought bread should be in the fridge: the preservatives in this bread are ideal for keeping that loaf in the refrigerator. The cool environment helps prevent mold and dryness.

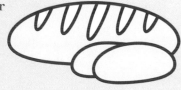

258. ONLY ORGANIC?

When it comes to buying organic food, it can cost more to buy all organic versus the price of conventional groceries. The key to save is to prioritize what's really important. When it comes to fruits and vegetables, if there's a peel on it that you're not eating, it's less important to go organic. This includes produce like bananas, mangoes, and watermelon. On the other hand, fresh food like milk, meat, and poultry should go on your priority organic list. Lastly, if the item is a snack, cereal, or frozen food, it's not critically important to go organic, as they are processed and less likely to have any trace chemicals on the food.

259. LOST AND FOUND

When grocery shopping, if you change your mind about buying something and don't feel like returning it to where you found it, still bring it to the checkout line with you. Many people will leave unwanted items in places where they don't belong—like a box of cereal with paper goods. Over time, misplaced items can get lost or damaged, or they can expire, leading to food waste. At the checkout, stores have a system in place to reshelf goods.

260. OIL SPILL

It happens: that bottle of olive oil has gone rancid. While you may not be able to cook or make a salad dressing with it anymore, it doesn't mean you still can't use it. Old olive oil is a fantastic conditioner for leather furniture. Just rub it all over the cracked, dried leather and let it sit for 30 minutes. Then buff away the excess with a clean towel to reveal furniture that's supple and soft. The same can be done with leather shoes; just a little goes a long way to turn dull leather shoes into a polished pair.

261. GRANDE GARDEN

One of the best things you can do for healthy soil in your garden is to create a habitat that worms love to be in. And just like you love your morning cup of joe, worms love coffee grounds. Scatter your used grounds in the garden and they'll do a few things: attract worms (who will make your soil richer over time) and release nutrients like nitrogen, calcium, phosphorous, and potassium into the ground. Simply scatter the grounds, work them into the soil a little bit, and you'll have a thriving garden!

262. STUCK ON YOU

It may seem harmless, but those little stickers you find on fruits and vegetables can wreak havoc on drains and wastewater-treatment plants. Before washing fruits and veggies, take the time to remove the stickers and put them into the trash. When they accidentally get washed down the drain, their adhesive can stick inside drains and pipes. If they get past that, they get caught in screens and filters at water treatment plants. It may not seem like a big deal, but if you think about the amount of produce that's stickered, it adds up.

263. PEEL OFF THE PACKAGING

When shopping for produce that needs to be stored at room temperature (like potatoes, onions, tomatoes, and bananas), take them out of the packaging they come in when you store them at home. These types of produce need air to circulate around them to prevent them from ripening too quickly. A ripening gas called ethylene can build up in packaging (even if it's perforated) and create food spoilage much more quickly.

264. FANTASTIC TAKEOUT

If you want to avoid disposable containers when you bring leftovers home from the restaurant, try transferring food into a container yourself. Bringing your own reusable container to the restaurant allows you to bring home your remaining dish the green way. Because most restaurants are unable to transfer food to your containers due to health code rules anyway, doing it yourself is no problem, and you can control what kind of containers you use.

265. SAVE THE WHALES

If you want to help save the whales, you should give up eating lobster. This is according to the advocacy group Seafood Watch, who says the ropes used for lobster fishing can "entangle critically endangered North Atlantic right whales." With just a few hundred whales left, they face near extinction unless changes happen quickly. While efforts are underway to identify "whale-safe lobster"—which are crustaceans harvested with ropes—the best bet to help now is to avoid or severely limit your lobster intake.

266. THE SALTY TRUTH

Microplastics are unfortunately everywhere, and it's important to do our part to help reduce usage and disposal of them into our waterways and environment. If you're looking to reduce your personal intake of microplastics, you should consider avoiding sea salt in your diet. A study in Spain tested 21 brands of sea salt and all of them tested positive for microplastics. It makes sense: sea salt is literally manufactured using salty water from waterways. Try table salt instead.

267. BUY IN SEASON

It just makes sense to buy fresh fruit and vegetables during the season in which they would naturally grow in your area. For example, local stores will always have lower prices on tomatoes and corn in the summer months, because quantities of this perishable produce are much higher. And strawberries are more expensive in January because it's winter, when berries aren't in season. Buy an ample supply of what you love in season, and then freeze what remains to ensure you always have peak produce ready to go for stir-fries and smoothies.

268. DON'T LIE

When we weigh our own produce, it's up to us to type in the right code for what we're bagging. So even though conventionally grown tomatoes are cheaper, don't bag organic ones and try to save money by using the nonorganic code at the scale or register. Supermarkets keep track of sales of products, and if they see organic tomatoes aren't selling, they'll stop stocking them. And it's important for us, as consumers, to support and buy organic fruits and vegetables so stores not only stock them but also so farmers keep growing them.

269. BULK BENEFITS

A simple and easy way to save money at the health food store is to take advantage of the bulk bin section. According to the Bulk Green Council, organic bulk foods cost about 89 percent less than buying the same item in packaged form. Because bulk bins do not have excessive packaging, the consumer can reduce their plastic purchases by buying in bulk. Generally, bulk items like nuts, flours, spices, grains, and other pantry/kitchen staples are a greener option to buy because less packaging also means more can be transported on trucks, which means less fuel is wasted. And no disposable paper and cardboard packages have to be made, so forests and energy are saved, too!

270. SO FISHY

Many of us incorporate salmon into our diets as a high-protein addition toward living a healthier lifestyle. But not all salmon fillets are the
same. Wild-caught Alaskan salmon have been found by scientists to
have high levels of heart-healthy omega-3s, are low in contaminants,
and are also caught sustainably through tough Alaskan regulations
and government monitoring of the fishing industry. Farm salmon, on
the other hand, are "grown" in tightly packed pools where diseases
are prevalent, so they are often fed high amounts of antibiotics, while
other varieties can contain high levels of chemicals and contaminants. So when choosing your next salmon dish, think wild instead
of farm-raised.

271. FORGET FROZEN

With nearly anything available to purchase online and have shipped
to your home, you might want to reconsider ordering anything that
comes packaged in dry ice. While freshly churned ice creams, seafood, and other items that need to stay frozen when shipped are tempting to order, it's the waste and disposal of dry ice that's problematic.
It turns out that dry ice—or solidified carbon dioxide—is incredibly
difficult to dispose of. Pouring it down drains can cause pipes to
freeze and burst. And the container, gloves, and anything else used
to hold or handle it need to be disposed of at a household hazardous
waste site. Instead, buy local and skip icy cold foods altogether with
online shopping.

272. SHOP LOCAL

Two reasons to shop for groceries from local merchants and not big box stores: you're supporting your local economy, and you'll likely cut back on single-use plastic. It turns out supermarket chains have a habit of excessively wrapping their fresh produce in single-use plastic. It helps keep produce fresher longer but also protects it from the hundreds of customers who handle the perishable products. Local stores are likely to use a lot less plastic, which gives you the option to stock up without the waste.

273. NO MORE MOLD

The Food and Drug Administration legally allows up to a whopping 60 percent of canned or frozen berries to contain mold and still be sold in a supermarket. While many berries are perfectly fine to eat, to be absolutely sure your berries are free from mold, go fresh instead. When strawberries, raspberries, and blackberries are in season, freeze them on a flat cookie sheet and store them in airtight containers. Only then do you know they are 100 percent free of mold.

274. LAST LONGER

If you've got a bumper crop of avocadoes (or picked up a bunch at the store on sale), there is one simple thing you can do to help slow down the ripening process. First, choose avocadoes that are not fully ripened—still green, firm, and definitely not soft to the touch. Place those avocadoes in the refrigerator, where the cool temperatures significantly slow down the ripening process to give the fruit a few extra days of shelf life. When you do think you might want an avocado, take it out of the fridge and leave it at room temperature for a full day. Enjoy!

275. BIG SAVER

Do you want to save money on organic and healthy food products? It turns out that when a new flavor or product just doesn't work at a regular retailer, the food manufacturer has to figure out what to do with the surplus. And a growing number of "grocery outlet" stores are selling these items at ridiculously low prices. While the selection may always be changing and inconsistent, the deals on certified organic and all-natural products can be incredible. Just google "grocery outlet near me" to find one to scope out.

276. UNJUNK FOOD

Not only can microwave popcorn be expensive, it also is wasteful and potentially dangerous: the nonstick coating inside the bag contains PFOA, a likely carcinogen, according to the Environmental Protection Agency. Instead, buy popcorn kernels from the bulk bin at the supermarket. It's significantly cheaper, and you can pop it on the stovetop in about the same time it takes to microwave popcorn. Plus, you can make as little or as much as you want and get creative with seasoning!

277. EGG-CELLENT IDEA

When buying eggs, the best style of carton to get them in is cardboard boxes and not plastic or Styrofoam. And while cardboard is widely recycled, egg cartons made from paperboard are actually not accepted in most recycling programs. The reason is this: it's made from the weakest recycled fibers and is basically in its final usage. Instead of tossing the carton in the trash, you can tear it up and compost it or add it to your food scraps collection if your community collects organic matter. Or, if you know someone with chickens, save them so they can use them.

278. CITRUS SPARKLE

Here's a simple and smart way to upcycle your old orange peels: make them into an eco-friendly household cleaner. Fill a glass jar with white vinegar and place the peels from about 3 to 4 oranges inside the jar. Let it sit for 7 to 10 days, strain the liquid, and use the orange-infused vinegar as an all-purpose cleaner all around the house (transfer it to a spray bottle). The white vinegar acts like a natural disinfectant and the natural oils from the citrus work as a degreaser. It also smells great, too!

279. PAST DUE

Overripe fruits and vegetables can often feel wasteful if you don't get around to eating them in time. But just because something is a little too mushy doesn't mean it isn't edible anymore. Overripe berries can be frozen and saved for later to be used in smoothies or pureed into a berry sauce for dessert toppings. Things like carrots, celery, mushrooms, and corncobs can be simmered into delicious broth. And squishy tomatoes are perfect candidates to be made into homemade sauces that can be canned or frozen in freezer bags to be used for later. You can even freeze overripe tomatoes by grating them on a box grater and storing in the freezer; just cook with them later when you want to add "fresh" tomatoes to a dish.

CHAPTER 4

SUPPORTING THE NATURAL WORLD

Those who know me—and really anyone who's just met me—know that I am a HUGE animal lover. I'll be on the floor playing with your dog sometimes before I even spit out a proper hello. I consider members of the animal world to be the ultimate innocents, and therefore it's our job to protect them. I know I'm far from alone in this. But the fact is, we negatively affect wildlife and our domesticated companions without even knowing we're doing it—and certainly without intending to do harm.

Awareness leads to action, and I hope these tips lead to both.

280. GOLD-FRESH

While we know filtered water is good for us to drink, have you thought about it for your pet goldfish? Tap water can have high levels of chlorine and ammonia, which is often used in water-treatment plants. This can affect the PH levels of the water, which affects the quality of living for fish. So using filtered water in fish tanks can help our aquatic friends live a healthier, happier life.

And when it's time to change the water, don't toss the old water down the drain. Like nutrient-dense compost, wastewater from fish is rich in nutrients, good bacteria, and other beneficial ingredients plants love.

281. THAT'S SPICY

There are many unusual and clever tricks to keep squirrels from raiding the bird feeder in your backyard. But one simple trick may actually work with no chemicals at all: use red pepper flakes. Rodents like squirrels hate the spicy, sharp taste of red paper flakes and quickly learn to avoid stealing the seeds. Our feathered friends, on the other hand, can't detect heat from red paper flakes and will devour it up along with the seed. The plus side is this: even if any animal ingests red pepper flakes, they may not like it, but it won't hurt them, either. You can also change the seed to safflower seeds (from a thistle-type flower), which are sold at home improvement stores and are a type of seed birds love but squirrels hate.

282. LIGHTS OUT

According to The Audubon Society, exterior lights turned on at night are light pollution for animals like migrating birds. The artificial light spatially disorients the birds and gives them a false horizon when flying at night. Often, birds will fly toward backlit windows in order to correct their flight, ultimately ending in their death. At least 100 million birds are killed every year by exterior lights. How to help? Turn off your exterior lights between midnight and dawn (peak migration hours for birds) and close your blinds and drapes to keep the interior lights on. Use timers if physically turning on and off lights becomes tiresome.

283. NO SWEET TWEETS

Did you know that birds have a taste for artificial sweeteners? The chemically overtly sweet taste of the pink and blue packets is very appealing to our feathered friends, once they get a taste for the saccharine sweetener—so much so that many birds will swipe them from outdoor tables at restaurants. Unfortunately, birds are the last animals that need to lose weight, so the zero nutritional content they get from consuming artificial sweeteners will fill them up but prevent them from gaining any nutritional benefit from their snacks. Some birds can even starve to death once they get fixated on sugar packets. Keep the packets away when you dine and ask restaurants to stash them away to help birds maintain their natural diet.

284. GOOD INTENTIONS, BAD RESULTS

Here's an old wives' tale to avoid: do not leave dryer lint outdoors in the hopes birds will pick it up and use it to feather their nest. Dryer lint contains chemical detergents from your clothes that can irritate birds and cause harm; even eco-friendly laundry detergent can irritate their sensitive skin and feathers. If you want to help birds, you can leave piles of dried grass (untreated with chemical fertilizers or pesticides), hair clumps (human, horse, and dog fur, also untreated), and the good old basics: twigs, moss, and pine needles. Just leave them close to wherever you think birds may find them, and they'll weave them into a nest for their young.

285. ZAP THE ZAPPERS

It's tempting to install bug zappers, those electric bug lights that "zap" mosquitoes at night when spending time outdoors. While they are effective at killing blood-thirsty mosquitoes, they also attract thousands of harmless insects, too. These insects are food for animals like birds, bats, and even aquatic wildlife, and they help keep the biodiversity of the forest intact. Because bug zappers don't know the difference between beneficial insects and pests, they can do more harm than good. So, zap the zappers and instead bring an electric fan outdoors. The breeze from the fan is usually enough to keep mosquitoes away.

286. WATER WISE

Sure, plastic dog bowls for food and water may seem like a safe and shatterproof way to take care of the family dog (especially if it picks up the bowl with its mouth), but they aren't the healthiest choice. Over time, they get scratched up, and small crevices can harbor harmful bacteria and germs. A better choice is to invest in stainless steel bowls, which can be sanitized easily with just equal parts baking soda, warm water, and salt. But a warning: while bleach can sanitize, never use it to clean your pet bowl, as they eat and drink from them.

287. PLANT FOR POLLINATORS

The National Wildlife Federation says the best way to attract and help wild animals thrive in your own yard is to bring in native plants that are part of your geographic region. The reason is simple: these plants are well adapted to thrive in your area, based on "the climate, soils, rainfall and availability of pollinators and seed dispersers." Your local wildlife species—from birds to butterflies and small to large mammals—will welcome these plants, which can serve an important role in the ecosystem. Visit nwf.org to find the top 10 plants for your region on their website.

288. A CLEAN CRUSH

Soda and beer in aluminum cans is a greener option than plastic bottles; metal can be recycled infinitely, but care must be taken when recycling them. Any residual liquid inside aluminum cans intensifies when they dry out; the strong smell of sugar or beer is too tempting for wildlife. What's more, the razor-sharp edges of the can's opening can also harm wild animals. Before recycling, simply rinse out the inside of the can and crush it. And consider using a recycling bin with a tight-fitting lid rather than a plastic bucket to keep curious critters out for good.

289. BEES LOVE THE BLUES

There's one simple thing you can do to help support critical honeybee colonies: plant more blue- and violet-colored flowers. Researchers have found that honeybees are naturally attracted to blue- and purple-hued flowers and produce more nectar as a result. Over time, bees have naturally preferred certain colors over others, and blue and purple flowers in their natural habitats are the clear winners. And as always: never use chemical insecticides and fertilizers in your garden when planting these deep-hued flowers.

290. DO GOOD AND GIVE RIGHT

If you want to support your local animal shelter, make sure you're donating items they actually need and not creating a burden for them. Items like an open bag of dog food, old toys, human personal care products like shampoo, crates, and carrying cases and even stacks of newspaper are not only unwanted but can cost the shelter money. These items are not needed for their rescue animals or the shelters, who are forced to dispose of them. The time it takes to throw away these items costs money and manpower, which can be used to help animals. If you want to donate, visit your local shelter and ask for a shopping list.

291. FEATHERED FRIENDS

It's important to make efforts to make sure our feathered friends avoid colliding with windows at our home. There are many things you can do, but one key thing, when placing a birdbath or a bird feeder outside, is to keep it at least 30 feet away from windows. This is the minimum length to prevent confusing reflections in the window. You can also cover the outside of the window with one-way transparent film; it lets you see outside, but it creates an opaque finish on the outside.

292. NATURAL DETERRENT

The next time you go for an exhausting workout at the gym, consider not washing your sweat-soaked workout clothes and smelly socks. The reason? They can be used to help discourage a wild animal from nesting under your home. Wild animals like foxes like to create den sites under porches, decks, or in sheds. And while it may be tempting and easy to scare them off with chemicals or traps, you can actually scare them naturally with your scent. Leaving garments that reek of the human scent can often be enough to deter them from turning your home into their home.

293. SNIP IT

Believe it or not, one of the most dangerous things your pet can eat isn't a food at all: it's the actual bag that your favorite chips or snack food comes packaged in. Even if you finish a bag of snack chips, the lingering smell still stays in the bag. And if you leave the bag where your dog—or a curious dumpster-diving critter—can find it, they'll naturally want to stick their head in. An entire Facebook page called "Prevent a Pet Suffocation" reports many animals actually suffocate to death when they trap themselves in the bag and are unable to breathe. To prevent this, simply cut the bag open on both ends and toss it into the trash.

294. MOUSE IN THE HOUSE

Some of the most common entry points for mice entering your home include where outside utility pipes or wires come into your home, if there's any rot or deterioration of your home's siding or if there are cracks along the foundation. Take the time to do an inspection outside your home to see if you have any of these, and seal them up. One

thing you can do if you think a mouse is entering your home through an entry point is to sprinkle baby powder on the ground; if you see tracks, that's an entry point that needs to be sealed up.

295. DON'T STRAY

If you see a cat and wonder if it's stray or feral, there's one thing you can do: check out its ears. Often, when a cat is neutered, a painless procedure is done to its right ear that gives it a small notch or tip. It's designed to inform anyone that this cat has in fact been neutered, is likely not feral, and has a home. If a cat does not have a notch, there is a high likelihood it's a stray, and you can contact a local shelter to help capture him.

296. PET PROJECT

The quality of dry pet food can quickly deteriorate if not properly stored. Look for tough plastic, glass, or metal bins with lids to keep pet food fresh; it also helps keep out rodents and insects. But do not transfer the food from the bag into the bin; keep the food in the original bag *inside* the bin. The reason is that pet food bags are designed to keep out moisture and light and can be an added layer of protection for the food. The general rule of thumb with pet food is that after you've opened the bag (and placed it in a bin), it should be used up within 6 weeks.

297. DEBUNKING BIODEGRADABLE

When shopping for party goods, you may be tempted to get something marketed as "biodegradable" balloons. The reality is that these latex balloons may degrade, but it can take up to 4 years for them to properly degrade all the way down. In those 4 years, the small pieces of latex can still end up as "food" ingested by wildlife. Plus, if these balloons were released with strings attached, the nylon ribbon string could tangle and strangle animals, too.

298. SEASHELLS BY THE SEASHORE

Is it okay to take shells from a beach? The overwhelming consensus from environmental groups is a resounding no. It's obvious that spiral-style shells are important to leave because they are literally homes for aquatic creatures. But even broken shells should be left in their place by the water. Many aquatic species use broken shells as armor or camouflage in the ocean, and birds often build nests with them.

299. LAWNMOWING GPS

Yes, there is a right way to mow the lawn so you can achieve a beautiful yard without causing harm to wildlife. It's simple: start by mowing from the center of your lawn and working slowly out. This movement gives wildlife of all sizes time to notice the disturbance and run outward away from your lawn mower. Working on the outer edges of the lawn and working in can force wildlife to run toward the center, where they can find themselves stuck with no escape.

300. A SAFE DRIVE

Your dog may love taking a ride in the car with you, but the American Humane Society says there are some rules to make sure they're safe when you drive. First, never let a dog ride in the back of a pickup truck; the organization estimates nearly 100,000 dogs die when a truck suddenly stops or swerves. And as much as they love it, try to limit the amount of time they stick their heads out of the window. The nonprofit says, "Wind can seriously irritate mucous membranes and blow pieces of grit into their eyes."

301. ROCK ON

It may seem harmless, but it's actually illegal to take rocks out of national parks. With millions of people visiting our parks, if everyone took a small natural souvenir home, it could have a devastating effect on the park. If caught, not only could you be charged with a federal crime, but it could also result in a hefty fee. Even stacking rocks in parks is frowned upon; it disrupts the natural biodiversity and creates an eyesore. After all, the true art is what Mother Nature has already created, so let the rocks be.

302. LOST AND FOUND

Here's a $10 investment that could be the most valuable thing you do for your cat or dog: get them microchipped. The tiny microchip is inserted in the back of the neck and is unique to your pet; if they get lost, it identifies who the owner is so they can be reunited with you. Plus, lost pets that have a microchip can be part of an emergency alert. Animal shelters in the area will be immediately notified of your pet's details, and you will have 24/7 free live support to help find your lost companion.

303. MAGIC TAPE

Butterflies are important pollinators, so anything you can do to help them thrive in your garden is a step in the right direction. If you ever see a butterfly that is slow-moving or helpless due to a torn wing, you can actually help them. A tiny piece of transparent tape can help repair a torn wing, enough to mend it and let them fly again. This will add a few extra valuable days to their life span, which could be enough for them to reproduce.

304. TOURIST TRAP

Did you know it's illegal to take sand from beaches in Hawaii? And it's also illegal to purchase sand online if it's taken from Hawaii. The reason is an uptick in erosion that is causing Hawaiian beaches to shrink. It's easy to understand why this sand is for sale: it's colorful, it's unusual, and it comes from a breathtaking destination. If you do see sand for sale online, report it to help get the listing removed. And always remember—even small amounts in your shoes and bags should be shaken out and left on the beach wherever you go.

305. TURTLE TIME

Ever see a large turtle in the middle of the road and wonder if you should help relocate it before it gets smashed by a car? Some tortoises can hurt you—like a snapping turtle—so care must be taken to make sure you don't get hurt. Wildlife experts agree that if you can safely help, you should. Use something like a floor mat from your car and nudge the turtle onto it. Then drag it backward (so the turtle is not facing you) across the road until the turtle is somewhere safe and sound.

306. SLICK IDEA

Do you want to prevent wasps and hornets from building a nest on your house? Instead of reaching for chemical insecticides, just fill a spray bottle with soap and water (using a biodegradable soap like castile soap for this). Then spray away. This simple method works because the soapy mixture clogs the breathing pores of insects and also creates a slick surface that can break down the nest. The residual soap on the surface also makes it slippery enough to prevent a new nest from being built in its place.

307. BE SMART ABOUT SOUVENIRS

When you're on a vacation at a faraway exotic destination, just remember this one rule: just because it's for sale, that doesn't mean it's legal to bring it back to the United States. The World Wildlife Fund warns travelers that it's illegal to purchase items made from many animal skins and byproducts. Things to avoid include any furs and feathers, turtle shell (usually combs and jewelry), ivory, medicines made from rhino horns and tiger bones, and even wool shawls and scarves called "Shahtoosh," woven from endangered Tibetan chiru antelope. When in doubt, just don't buy it.

308. WOOD YOU?

When a tree falls in your yard, do you make plans to immediately clean it up? If you have the ability to let it go and leave it be, do it. A fallen tree serves as shelter for animals and also can be a buffet of food for critters and wildlife. And as the tree continues to decay, its nutrients are broken down and enrich the soil. And even in fire-prone areas, fallen trees can act as a deterrent because the large trunk and branches are less flammable due to its density.

309. HUMANE SOCIETY

According to Oxford University's Wildlife Conservation Research Unit, there are tourist traps around the world that exploit wild animals in the hopes you'll visit and participate. If you want to avoid supporting animal cruelty, be on the lookout for these excursions when you travel abroad, and avoid them at all costs. They include riding with elephants, taking selfies with any animal, performing and swimming with dolphins, and holding wild animals like sea turtles and dancing monkeys. If it doesn't feel natural or right, it probably isn't.

310. BEE-UTIFUL TIP

One of the easiest ways to help vulnerable bee populations is to give them a safe, dry place to live in your backyard. A stack of firewood is a natural and untreated place that's perfect for bees. All you have to do is use a cordless drill and create holes on the sides of the stacked firewood between 2 and 10 millimeters in width. Just drill as deep as the drill bit will go and randomly create tunnels on the side of the firewood. Don't go all the way through; bees like a closed tunnel. And sand away any splinters and rough edges because bees prefer a smooth entry.

311. EASY EVICTION

Many people like to hang a wreath on the front door to decorate the front of their house. But many birds mistake the wreath for a potential place to nest and call home. If this happens to you, you have options. You could leave the birds be, or, if you don't want them nesting, you can try this gentle trick to nudge them away: Embed some magnets inside the wreath. The natural magnetic field can be disruptive to birds, making the wreath an uninhabitable place. Don't worry, it doesn't hurt them; it just annoys them and makes them want to go away. It's hidden and safe, and it keeps your wreath nest-free.

312. LIGHTS OUT!

If you're visiting Florida when millions of freshly hatched sea turtles are making their way to the ocean, you can do just one thing to help them out: turn off the lights. The baby turtles make their way to water at night using the light of the moon to guide the way. But when outdoor lights (or even bright lights coming from inside the home) are brighter than the moon, they often head toward those illuminated sources. And when they go in the wrong direction, it can often lead to their demise. Turn off the lights and spread the word if you find yourself in Florida during June through November.

313. D'OH, A DEER

According to the Humane Society of the United States, one of the biggest mistakes good-hearted people make is they assume a baby deer found alone must be an orphan. But the truth is if the fawn is calm and lying down quietly, the odds are the mother is not too far away. The mother usually visits her baby a few times a day and will likely not appear unless you're gone. Unless the fawn is crying or wandering alone, there's no need to contact a wildlife rehabilitator.

314. NO HONEY

Some DIY bird feeder projects call for rolling pine cones or fruit in honey and then coating the entire outside with birdseed as a decorative way to feed our feathered friends. This DIY should be avoided at all costs. While honey is natural, it's not a good choice for birds to consume. The reason is that honey is an easy material for bacteria and mold growth, and those can be fatal to birds. Instead, stick with birdseed that's fresh and clean if you do want to feed birds in your backyard.

315. HELPING KERMIT

Did you know that male frogs spend the winter months in the muddy part of the pond underwater, breathing through their skin? During this time, the biggest threat to these frog fellows is often organic debris—like dead plants and leaves—that can decay under ice and release gasses that can kill the frogs. To help, take the time to remove excess debris out of the pond and place that organic matter into a compost or on solid land to naturally decompose. And do one more thing: float a baseball on the water. This will prevent ice from totally sealing over the pond this winter.

316. HAPPY DOG

Many of us love our family dog so much, we don't see it as a problem when they jump in the backyard pool to go for a swim. But the reality is your dog's ears, nose, and eyes are more sensitive than ours, and the chlorine in the pool may actually harm them in the long run. To be on the safe side, look for non-chlorine chemicals like bromine to keep your pool clean and safe. It's also a good idea to rinse them off with fresh water from the garden hose to wash off the excess pool chemicals to prevent from drying on their skin and fur.

317. FELINE FRIENDS

Nearly four *billion* birds are killed every year by household cats. While it's instinctual for cats to hunt, these numbers can be devastating to bird populations. Some folks assume that putting a bell or brightly colored collar on their cat will allow the birds to sense the cats' presence before it's too late. But the National Wildlife Federation says to not use this old trick; a bell isn't "something that wildlife associates with predators or danger." And most birds don't see color, so these collars are totally ineffective. The best preventative measure? Keep your cats indoors.

318. DOGGY DAYCARE

Man's best friend also needs protection from the sun's harsh rays. If you're planning to spend a lot of time outdoors with your dog, consider applying sunscreen to their snout. Given that their coat acts as a natu- ral sun protection barrier, it's the nonfur areas—like the snout and exposed parts of the dog's underbelly—that need SPF the most. But be sure to choose a sunscreen that has no zinc oxide. This chemical is toxic to animals, so check labels very carefully.

319. BETTER BIRDSEED

Many of us like to buy suet balls or bird food that is encapsulated in mesh bags (which helps keep the birdseed together when you hang it outside). While for the most part our feathered friends can get a healthy meal or snack from these, there is a chance they can get entangled in the mesh bags. When the suet or bird food gets low, it creates air pockets around the mesh bag. This can cause birds to dig deeper into the bag for food, which can lead to their legs and beaks getting trapped and entangled. It's best to avoid feeding birds with mesh bags and to stick with traditional methods that involve loose feed instead.

320. TOXIC TENNIS

Do you buy tennis balls to play fetch with your dog? Turns out the fuzzy exterior isn't good for them or the environment. The soft, fuzzy coating is actually plastic, and when it sheds, it's a microplastic that can end up in our waterways and also your dog's digestive system. An alternative is to purchase "plastic-free tennis balls," which have the same bounce, shape, and feel of the conventional balls but are totally free of microplastics.

321. POUND PRESENTS

The Environmental Protection Agency estimates the average American throws away about 70 pounds of textiles every year. While many of us know lightly worn clothes can be easily donated to charities like Goodwill and The Salvation Army, what do you do with old bath towels, worn sheets, and blankets? Give them a good wash in the washing machine and donate them to your local animal shelter. Given that many pound puppies and cats have to sleep on concrete floors or cold metal cages, any warmth from old bedding, blankets, and towels will be put to good use. And while you're at it, pick up some meat-based baby food at the supermarket: shelters use this food to feed highly malnourished animals in an effort to nurse them back to health.

322. FLOWER POWER

If you want to live in harmony with wildlife but also want a yard full of beautiful flowers, consider blossoms that look great but are unpalatable to animals. Daffodils are winners because they flourish and are detested by squirrels, rabbits, and deer because of their foul taste. Other types of naturally deterring flowers include alliums (anything from the onion family), hyacinths, and geraniums, which can all be planted at the borders of gardens to act as repellents and prevent animals from dining on the flowers they love.

323. BE A BAT MAN

It turns out bats are critical for keeping our ecosystem in check. According to a published study in the journal *Science*, bats eat so many insects they save the United States agriculture industry over $3 billion per year as natural pest control. Unfortunately, bats are at risk for a number of reasons, but there are things you can do to help. Start by eliminating pesticides from your own yard; a single bat can eat up to 3,000 insects per night. Turn off lights at night because a dark environment is how bats thrive and see best. And finally, leave dead and dying trees be; the inside of these fallen giants make a natural habitat for bats.

324. QUICK CLEANUP

With backyard summer barbecues and picnics in full swing during the hot summer months, be sure that even the smallest food scraps from your meal are packed up and taken with you. Even tiny specks of bread scraps can become a tasty meal for birds, but they can go stale, become moldy, and harm birds quickly after your festivities. Anything with chocolate—think brownies, candy bars, and dessert toppings—can also be harmful to birds because chocolate contains the chemical theobromine, which is a toxin to birds (and dogs and cats, too). Generally, if humans can eat it, birds can't. So be diligent in cleaning up after any outdoor party.

325. FORGET FLEAS

According to the Humane Society of the United States, over 1,600 pets died as a result of toxins from flea treatments, so finding natural ways to prevent and kill fleas is important if your pet is like a member of your family. Prevention and common sense can go a long way. Vacuuming carpets, rugs, and furniture where your pet lives, along with regularly washing their bedding in hot water, can help prevent flea infestations. And real lavender essential oil can also help for dogs: Add some to a natural flea soap and let the mixture sit on your pup's coat for 10 minutes during bath time.

326. CLEAN SWEEP

Birdhouses offer an excellent way to help our feathered friends with shelter to raise their brood, but these houses need to be cleaned every year; parasites and bacteria could be living inside. Autumn is an excellent time to do this. The first step is to remove the old nest inside the birdhouse (while wearing rubber gloves); you can leave it in the forest to decompose naturally. Then use a diluted mixture of 1 part bleach to 9 parts hot water and spray the inside and outside of the birdhouse to disinfect it; scrub with a sponge. In a sunny spot, place the birdhouse to fully dry out for a full 24 hours. Then reinstall and wait for a bird to discover it and make it their new home.

327. DRIVER'S ED

Driving at night can also mean the possibility of hitting a wild animal on the road. To avoid this, there are a few simple steps you can take when driving. The obvious is to slow down and drive the speed limit; slowing down a little bit gives you extra time to brake and avoid a collision. Look for "eye shine" or glowing eyes in the distance to help identify wildlife ahead on the road. And remember: Many wild animals often travel in herds—especially deer and wild turkeys—so if you spot one, be cautious of others nearby.

328. SUPER SHELTER

According to the National Wildlife Federation, fall is a good time to rake up leaves and let them become shelter for wildlife. Just leave a section of your yard with raked-up leaves a few inches deep and wet it down if it's a little too dry and might blow away. It'll eventually become the perfect shelter for small animals like salamanders, chipmunks, turtles, and shrews, or even be home to beneficial insects like earthworms. Even caterpillars will leave their pupae there, and that will become a food source for birds come spring.

329. BEE CAREFUL

Bees are important to our world because they help with the pollination of flowers and crops, but being bothered by bees while outdoors can be a pesky situation. If this is a concern for you, instead of using an insect-killing spray, why not make a natural bee-repellant spray? Simply fill a reusable spray bottle with witch hazel oil and add a few drops of tea tree oil. Shake and spray the solution on your skin whenever you go outdoors and don't want to be bothered by bees. The medicinal smell from the witch hazel oil is obnoxious to bees and other insects, making this spray an excellent way to keep them away from you … naturally.

330. FEEDING TIME

It's common knowledge that feeding bread to waterfowl is a terrible idea, and the reason is the same as it is for us: Bread offers little nutritional value and is high in carbohydrates. It's junk food for birds. When birds fill up on bread, not only do they gain excess weight and learn to become dependent on handouts from humans, they also become slower, which makes it harder for them to evade predators. If you enjoy feeding wild birds, opt for thawed-out frozen peas as a healthier alternative instead.

331. OH, DEER

If you live in a cold-weather climate where deer reside, there are things you can do to help them and things you should avoid at all costs. Feeding deer is one of the worst things you can do, especially giving them new food that isn't normally part of their diet, like alfalfa hay and corn. Unfortunately, new food "shocks" their system, and they are more likely to die if they overeat it. Instead, when you prune ornamental bushes and trees, leave the tender branches in piles where deer can find them. They'll eat what they want and will be able to digest it because it's part of their normal diet.

332. BITTER LITTER

If you've been flushing used cat litter down the toilet, stop. The Sierra Club says that a common organism found in kitty litter called Toxoplasma cannot be eliminated by traditional wastewater facilities, so it often ends up in waterways and can kill sea otters. The environmental group also recommends looking for bentonite-free litter because the mining of this common ingredient in kitty litter "tears up land surface." To dispose of litter, use a biodegradable bag to hold it and dispose in your regular garbage.

333. A BAD FIGHT

For many, backyard fun may include filling up balloons with water and having a water balloon fight. But when the balloons burst, fragments from the inflatable can end up being dispersed all over the yard. And often, these rubbery pieces are left where wild animals can mistake them for food and ingest them. Even with so-called "biodegradable" balloons, these materials can take up to 4 years to properly degrade. That still leaves plenty of time for wild animals to eat the pieces and end up harmed or dying. Instead of balloons, consider water guns: all of the fun and none of the waste.

CHAPTER 5

A WAY TO MAKE YOUR COMMUNITY STRONGER AND BETTER

Know what feels even better than doing good things for the environment? Joining in with others to make even more of an impact! Sometimes supporting a group cause or joining a team can just be all the more satisfying and enjoyable. I also find that by learning about what others are doing, I learn more in general. And knowledge, as always, is power.

There are so many ways to contribute what you can to eco-friendly team efforts. You can donate your time or money, for sure, but you can also borrow, barter, or simply pay it forward. Many hands make light work, as they say. I'd like to add: many hands make a lighter footprint, too.

334. SOAPY SOLUTIONS

Many of the world's preventable diseases could be curtailed simply with proper hand-washing. Clean the World is a nonprofit organization that is working with the hotel industry to collect used soap from hotel rooms; they boil and sanitize the soaps down into new bars of soap and distribute them all over the world to people in need. While the organization primarily works with hotels, they also will gladly accept bars of soap from people, too. So, if you've hoarded a whole collection of mini bars of hotel soaps, send them their way at cleantheworld.org.

335. VOLUNTEER MATCH GAME

If you want to support a worthy cause and find the right charity that could use your skills and time, check out the website volunteermatch.org. They've helped millions of people find places to volunteer by matching them with organizations that can use their skills "to create real impact." Search for opportunities in your city and scroll through specific listings based on date and charity type and then learn what the specific volunteer program needs from you.

336. BE A FREQUENT GIVER

There are more than $50 billion worth of loyalty points from airlines, hotel chains, and retailers given to customers every year. Yet, 30 percent of those points go unredeemed. The website PointWorthy .com connects people with nonprofit and charitable causes that they believe in so they can donate their unredeemed or unwanted loyalty points. Just search for your favorite charity, find out which loyalty points they accept, click, and give! It's that easy.

337. SHARE THE LOVE

If you have a wedding gown that's less than 5 years old or a unique vintage design that you'd like to donate to someone in need, consider the nonprofit Brides Across America. The organization accepts lightly used wedding gowns in all sizes (and accessories like veils and tiaras) and finds military brides in need to gift them to. The organization has been honored by First Lady Michelle Obama and Jill Biden for their efforts to support active military members. Learn more at bridesacrossamerica.com.

A WAY TO MAKE YOUR COMMUNITY STRONGER AND BETTER

338. BOUNTIFUL BAGS

Do you have a reusable bag overload? Perhaps you have bags you've received for free at the store, purchased too many, or were gifted a few. The great thing about reusable bags is that they cut down on waste and they can be used over and over again. So, try this with your extra bags: Fill them with goods your local food bank or shelter needs. Then they can reuse those bags and let patrons use them to fill up with food. You can also donate extra reusable bags to soup kitchens, shelters, and charities that need to carry and transport goods, too.

339. SPARE CHANGE THE WORLD

Whenever you buy a cup of coffee, a pair of shoes, or groceries, would you round up your purchase to the nearest dollar to help a worthy charity, too? The app CoinUp let's you do that and it's easy to use. Simply sync a credit card to the CoinUp app after you've installed it on your phone. If you buy a cup of coffee for $1.97, it'll automatically round up your purchase to $2 and donate the three cents to charity. You get to pick the charity that benefits and the CoinUp app gives you an update on how your spare change you've donated is helping to make a difference.

340. GIVE AND SAVE

Nonprofits like Goodwill are a great place to donate a whole variety of household items to be resold for charitable works. The list of accepted items is long and varied: it's everything from lightly used cookware to electronics to even cars in any condition. But when you donate, you can also write-off your donation as a tax deduction, too. To make it easy, Goodwill offers a "donation value guide" that generalizes what most items in a certain category are worth. For example, winter coats have a tax-deductible value of $12.99 and children's books are worth around 59 cents each. It all adds up in the name of good!

341. HOW BEAUTIFUL

If you have a stash of unused beauty products at home, why not donate them to help women in need? The nonprofit Project Beauty Share connects people with new products to give to women and families overcoming abuse, addiction, homelessness, and poverty. All items must be new, and most-wanted items include makeup bags, moisturizers, soap (both bar and body wash), fragrance, personal care items (like deodorants), clean makeup brushes, hair care, and nail polishes. Learn more at projectbeautyshare.org.

A WAY TO MAKE YOUR COMMUNITY STRONGER AND BETTER

342. GIVE SMARTER

Many of us like to donate used clothing to charity as a way to reduce waste and give back. When donating, be sure to launder clothing prior to giving and use a fragrance-free detergent so recipients who are sensitive to fragrance won't be affected. If you have a lot of one type of clothing (like kid's clothes), try to sort them to help the charity save time. Mark different bags with "kid's coats" or "T-shirts" and "bedding." And be sure to check all the pockets; charities like Goodwill report that many people accidentally leave credit cards and photo IDs in clothes they give.

343. SEE CLEARLY

Did you know hundreds of millions of people all over the world live with visual impairment that could be easily fixed with an eye exam and a pair of eyeglasses? The next time you need a pair of glasses, consider shopping with a brand or retailer that matches your purchase with a donated pair to someone in need. Brands like Warby Parker give a pair for free for every pair sold, which means when you're seeing better, someone else in the world is, too.

344. PAGE TURNERS

Even in an age of digital reading, printed books are still in demand and can be donated if you're ready to make room on your bookshelf at home. The rule of thumb for donating books is this: If the book is less than 2 to 3 years old based on when it was published, donate it to your local library, who will resell the book at a fundraiser to raise money for their valuable work. If it's older than that, donate it to a Salvation Army or Goodwill store, who will resell it in-store. Either way, if you donate them, be sure to get a receipt for tax deduction purposes.

345. GOOD DONATIONS

Perhaps you've heard this "tip" before: you can donate used toys to a local children's hospital. While it is true that many hospitals do have wish lists for toys, it's always for new and unwrapped toys, never used. The reason is that hospitals have very strict hygiene policies and can not accept even barely used toys. Before donating, check to see if your local hospital has a wish list or, even better, a registry where you can buy exactly what they need.

346. CANNED GOODS

Donating food to your local food bank is a great way to find a home for unexpired food. But keep in mind that just because it's technically food, it doesn't make it automatically okay to give. Generally, canned food that is unlabeled or has any rust on it is not okay to donate and should be tossed away in the trash. Plus, homemade food items, beverage mixes, and soda should also be avoided. The most-wanted items include healthy foods like canned and boxed meals (think mac and cheese), pasta, rice, cereal, canned fruits and vegetables, and cooking oil.

347. NO WIRE HANGERS!

It seems logical that if you have a lot of wire or plastic hangers at home, that a resell shop like The Salvation Army or Goodwill would want to use them because they sell a lot of clothes. Turns out, they don't want your hangers *unless* you have lightly used clothes to donate and hang on them as well. If you don't have clothes to donate alongside the hangers, bring your wire hangers back to the dry cleaner or bundle them together for recycling. And plastic hangers are a bit more difficult, so the next time you buy clothes, just leave the hanger behind at the store so they can reuse or recycle it.

348. SPICE OF LIFE

Here are some items your local food bank loves to get during the holiday season: spices. Essential spices like salt, pepper, chili powder, and cinnamon are essential; they can go a long way to make unseasoned food like rice, beans, and oatmeal taste a whole lot better.

349. VOLUNTEER VIRTUALLY

If you think donating your time to a charity means you need to physically be somewhere to help, think again. The rise in people working from home has resulted in virtual volunteer methods. The Smithsonian, for example, has a digital volunteer program that allows people to help transcribe documents related to their work. Amnesty International looks to volunteers to help flag abusive tweets against women politicians. And environmental organizations often need social-media-savvy volunteers to manage their accounts. There's so much you can do to help in just a few minutes a day.

A WAY TO MAKE YOUR COMMUNITY STRONGER AND BETTER

350. PERSONAL CARE

Ever wonder what to do with small personal electronics like hair dryers, flat irons, and curling irons when they no longer work? First, don't donate broken electronics to charities like Goodwill and the Salvation Army; they don't want them, and it costs them money to dispose of the goods. But the good news? They are easily recyclable.

The electronics chain Best Buy will take your broken personal care electronics and recycle them free of charge. Just bring them to the store and they'll handle the rest.

351. WIN WIN

Many of us will fill a bag with unwanted items and drop them off at Goodwill as a way to help the charity, clean out our closets, and feel better that our clothes are going anywhere but the landfill. While we may forgo the receipt for tax deduction purposes (because it can be laborious to itemize every single item donated), consider getting a receipt when donating larger items. Furniture, artwork, and working major electronics all retain value when donated, so research what their estimated retail value is and place a post-it note on each item when donating. You'll be able to deduct around 30 percent of that value from your taxes at the end of the year.

352. STAR SUPPLIES

During the start of the school year, there are donation drives to give students the essentials they need to excel at school. But the winter months are actually a critical time to donate things like binders, pencils, pens, folders, and notebooks, too. Having the right supplies is something that's needed nearly year-round, not just at the start of the school season. Local charities are also in need of in season items especially in cold climates like winter coats, hats, mittens, new warm socks, and blankets and towels. So, if you have lightly used school supplies or winter clothes clogging up your closet, save them from the trash and think about giving these things back to people who need them more.

353. ASK AHEAD

Donating food to a food bank is a great small step to help someone in need who faces food insecurity. Sometimes we end up donating our least-wanted items to the food bank, and other times we assume that holiday foods seem festive. But the next time, think about asking ahead to see what items the food bank needs most. What tops most in-demand ingredients are things like peanut butter, soup, and cereal. Calling ahead will ensure that your donation is making a real difference and going to good use somewhere outside your own pantry.

A WAY TO MAKE YOUR COMMUNITY STRONGER AND BETTER

354. BE THE CHANGE

Since 1987, the UNICEF program Change for Good has raised over $185 million through the collection of leftover foreign currency in-flight on international airlines and at airports and airport lounges around the world. If you have a collection of unwanted foreign currency, collect it all together and bring it with you the next time you fly. Any American Airlines Admirals Club Lounge (regardless of whether you are a member) will accept your spare change for the program. One hundred percent of the funds raised are used to help children all over the world in dire need. Learn more at unicef.org.

355. ALL THE MORE REASON

Whether it's cleaning up parks, planting trees, or walking dogs at the animal shelter, we know giving time can make a difference. But if you're still hesitating to donate your time for the greater good, consider that your actions are also tax-deductible. If you drive to volunteer, you can deduct 14 cents a mile and include tolls and parking on your personal income tax. Just make sure the charity you're working with is a registered 501(c)(3) charity in order to take advantage of the savings.

356. HUMANE HARDWARE

Did you stock up on home repair hardware only
to find it collecting dust? If DIY isn't your thing,
you can give your tools a new home by donating
them to your local Habitat for Humanity. The items
they desperately need the most are toolboxes, organizers, tool
bags, and tool belts for volunteers to use. Keeping their tools
organized and handy helps them move quickly from site to site.
Also, if you have drill bits and saw blades in any shape or size, those
are always in need. When bits and blades hit an old nail in the demo
or renovation work, it dulls them very quickly and they need to be
replaced often. Learn more at habitat.org

357. WONDERFULLY WEIRD

More than 20 million pounds of goods are donated to Goodwill stores
every single year, ranging from clothes to books to furniture. But
they also include what Goodwill refers to as "rogue" items, which are
the wacky, weird, and wild things. And while it may seem foolish to
donate something unconventional to Goodwill, they gladly take them
because they know collectors will pay a pretty penny for some of
your funkier items. So, even if it's weird to you, it's fundraising gold
to Goodwill and one less thing in the landfill. Think of it this way: one
man's weird trash is another's collectible treasure. But remember, if
it's soiled, broken, or recalled for safety reasons, dump it in the trash
and not in the Goodwill donation bin.

A WAY TO MAKE YOUR COMMUNITY STRONGER AND BETTER

358. PUPPY PICK-UP

Do you want to help your local animal shelter in some way beyond just writing a check? One way you can help is by being a transporter for animals. Many organizations often pull at-risk animals from kill shelters and need volunteers to pick them up and bring them to their shelter. They also need drivers to help bring adopted animals to vet appointments or for adopt-a-thons during high occupancy months. You can also help bring an adopted dog or cat to their new foster home. Just making a shelter aware of your travel plans can help connect the dots so they can use the location where you're going to help an animal in need.

359. PERFECT MATCH

Do you want to find the perfect volunteer opportunities in the community where you live? You can do it all online and search by zip code on the website VolunteerMatch.org The opportunities can be sorted by "in-person" or "virtual," by your skill level, cause areas, and more. A recent search for my town had requests for everything from watering native plants at a local sanctuary to delivering meals to people in need to helping blind dogs find their forever home.

360. THANKS BUT NO THANKS

If you're making a donation to a charity, be sure to tell them that you would like to opt out in receiving any free gift (a T-shirt, tote bag, etc.) or regular newsletter/magazine. These items are used as incentives to help raise money for the charity but cost money to make and ship. By opting out of receiving something you probably didn't want anyway, you can make sure the full value of your donation is going toward their good works.

361. WISE CHOICE

Be wary of donating clothes to those "drop off" donation boxes often found in supermarket parking lots. Yes, the clothes dropped in those bins are collected and recycled, but they are often designated for questionable for-profit companies that make money selling used clothes for textile recycling. It's best to donate to reputable charities—like Goodwill and The Salvation Army—where you know your donation will go to good use.

A WAY TO MAKE YOUR COMMUNITY STRONGER AND BETTER

362. MAKE A WISH

Did you know that most shopping malls that have water fountains that people toss coins into donate the spare change to charities? If you're raising money for a local nonprofit organization, it can be as easy as getting in touch with your local mall and picking up the coins. Your local bank can then arrange to ship the coins to the closest US Mint to be processed as part of the "Mutilated Coin Redemption Program." In just a few weeks, the amount will be wired and deposited into the charity's bank account. How easy is that?

363. LEAVE IT BEHIND

When shopping in grocery stores and when certain items like beans, pasta, and rice are in high demand, try to do one thing: avoid food items that are marked as a "WIC"-eligible item. WIC items are eligible for purchase by people on federal assistance, and they're limited to purchasing only those items in the store. If WIC items are sold out, then people on nutritional assistance have the potential to go home empty-handed. If you're able to purchase non-WIC items, do so! You're making sure that the people who need WIC items the most are able to get them and feed their families.

364. DOUBLE DUTY

On your next journey abroad, be sure to check out the website pack forapurpose.org. They allow you to "donate" a little extra space in your luggage by bringing items locals at your destination need. You can pack items like 400 pencils for a school, 5 deflated soccer balls with an inflation device, a stethoscope, blood pressure cuff, or 500 band-aids for a local hospital. Shipping these goods halfway around the world can be expensive, so just tossing them into your checked luggage can reduce emissions. And when you arrive at your destination, just find the local hotel or lodging facility that participates in the program and drop off your goods. It's that simple!

365. GIVE THE REST!

Sure, you can donate items like lightly used clothes, kitchenware, books, and other household items to Goodwill, but did you know you can also donate gift cards? No matter the amount left, you can donate unwanted gift cards to your local Goodwill store. Billions of dollars go unused every year on gift cards—even if there's only a few cents remaining—so grab all your remaining balanced gift cards and donate. The charity can look up the remaining balance on the cards and either re-sell them in stores or consolidate them to a third-party vendor who gives a percentage of the total balances to the nonprofit charity.

A WAY TO MAKE YOUR COMMUNITY STRONGER AND BETTER

ACKNOWLEDGMENTS

I CAN'T BELIEVE THIS IS MY 15TH BOOK. It boggles my mind that I've been writing books for nearly 30 years (I started when I was 18), and I honestly feel like I've hit the publishing lottery with the chance to put pen to paper and see each book come to life.

A big thank you to Joy Tutela, who has been my agent for as long as I can remember. I once had an idea to do a book that was one part entertaining and one part planner for . . . funerals. I called it *Happy Endings*. Joy nudged me in the right direction to put that idea in the "maybe" pile.

Universal Syndicate, thank you for publishing my syndicated column this whole time! You brought my strange but true words of eco wisdom to millions and now look at this! There's a book!

My editor at Countryman Press, Ann Treistman. Isabel McCarthy and everybody else for bringing this book to life.

The team at *Naturally, Danny Seo* magazine. It's been 10 years since we started publishing it? Time flies. Barry, Sandy, Alexis, Michael, Patti, Nancy, Jeremy, Bill, Yelena, Zoya, Joe, Christian, and all the contributors, too: Bobbi Brown, Catherine McCord, Rebecca Ffrench, Rikki Snyder, David Engelhardt, Jonas Jungblut, Jeffrey Hittner, Leslie Orlandini, Shelby Deering, and Olivia Roszkowski.

Drew Barrymore. You have an incredible platform and an even more incredible spirit. Thank you for . . . EVERYTHING.

Mr. Harry Connick Jr. Yes, folks, he is just as nice on camera and off. Thank you for the lovely foreword and for continuing to be an even more lovely friend.

Noelle Primavera has also been a rock in my life. Decades? A brilliant publicist, but also someone I treasure as a friend.

My family, my friends, and my rock in life—Kerry—thank you and I love you all.

To Kelli Lamb,

my business partner, my ride-or-die,

my fellow *Housewives* fanatic, and my friend.

Image Credits: Page 14: iStock.com / Valentina Antuganova; page 16: iStock.com / FingerMedium; page 18: iStock.com / Tanarch; pages 23, 119: iStock.com / Amanda Goehlert; pages 24, 54: iStock .com / Suesse; page 26: iStock.com / VanReeel; pages 30, 91, 124: iStock.com / kadirkaba; pages 33, 204: iStock.com / lushik; page 34: iStock.com / lesyau_art; page 37: iStock.com / bounward; page 41: iStock.com / roccomontoya; pages 43, 92: iStock.com / Anna Bova; pages 44, 51: iStock .com / Nadiinko; page 45: iStock.com / Stockyarder; pages 46, 95, 138, 180, 198: iStock.com / Turac Novruzova; pages 49, 197: iStock.com / Devita ayu Silvianingtyas; page 62: iStock.com / Rifai ozil; page 67: iStock.com / appleuzr; page 69: iStock.com / Satoshi Kikyo; page 71: iStock.com / Alona Stanova; page 72: iStock.com / LysenkoAlexander; page 77: iStock.com / VectorBird; pages 80, 177, 184: iStock .com / denkcreative; page 82: iStock.com / ngupakarti; page 84: iStock.com / Maksym Rudoi; page 89: iStock.com / Rudzhan Nagiev; page 99: iStock.com / RLT_images; page 100: iStock.com / Irina Samoylova; page 102: iStock.com / komunitestock; page 105: iStock.com / ONYXprj; page 109: iStock .com / bortonia; page 115: iStock.com / Elena Pimukova; page 117: iStock.com / mightyisland; page 120: iStock.com / mayrum; page 123: iStock.com / Yuliia Duliakova; page 126: iStock.com / rambo182; page 128: iStock.com / sabeiskaya; pages 129, 202: iStock.com / SirVectorr; page 132: iStock.com / Marina Akinina; page 134: iStock.com / Anton Shaparenko; page 136: iStock.com / Polina Tomtosova; page 139: iStock.com / Photoplotnikov; pages 142, 161, 181, 190, 201: iStock.com / JakeOlimb; page 143: iStock.com / anttohoho; page 146: iStock.com / calvindexter; page 147: iStock.com / PCH-Vector; page 151: iStock.com / grafikazpazurem; page 152: iStock.com / Catur Katamsi; page 157: iStock.com / vectorwin; page 164: iStock.com / Mariia Ronina; page 168: iStock.com / Polina Ekimova; page 170: iStock.com / artdee2554; page 172: iStock.com / sodafish; page 173: iStock.com / Illustrator de la Monde; page 191: iStock.com / Dimitris66; page 194: iStock.com / PinkyRabbit

Copyright © 2024 by Danny Seo Media Ventures
Foreword copyright © 2023 by Harry Connick Jr.

All rights reserved
Printed in the United States of America

For information about permission to reproduce selections from this book, write to
Permissions, Countryman Press, 500 Fifth Avenue, New York, NY 10110

For information about special discounts for bulk purchases, please contact
W. W. Norton Special Sales at specialsales@wwnorton.com or 800-233-4830

Manufacturing by Versa Press
Book design by Allison Chi
Production manager: Devon Zahn

Library of Congress Control Number: 2023946368

Countryman Press
www.countrymanpress.com

An imprint of W. W. Norton & Company, Inc.
500 Fifth Avenue, New York, NY 10110
www.wwnorton.com

978-1-68268-873-1

10 9 8 7 6 5 4 3 2 1